CHOICES

FROM CONFUSION TO CLARITY

SARAH LANE

Choices

First published in 2014 by

Panoma Press
48 St Vincent Drive, St Albans, Herts, AL1 5SJ, UK

info@panomapress.com
www.panomapress.com

Book layout by Neil Coe

Printed on acid-free paper from managed forests.

ISBN 978-1-909623-44-6

DEDICATION

To my 'Little Noodle' Nick

May you grow up knowing there are always choices in your life and feeling confident enough to make great ones.

TESTIMONIALS

"*Choices* provides a plethora of ideas to help us make the best ones. It's jam-packed with practical tools, which you can't fail to find helpful. Sarah has a wonderful way of weaving in stories to make you yearn to turn the page."

**Martyn Dicker, Director of HR & OD,
Fairtrade Foundation and fun-loving dad to baby Thilini**

...

"As a coach Sarah has a unique blend of subject passion, skill and intellect. This book allows Sarah to introduce her unique approach to a wider audience."

**Steve Thompson-Martyn,
Director CDL Consulting and rugby wizard**

...

"After reading *Choices*, I didn't see things through a new pair of eyes, I just stopped covering the perfectly good pair I had with rose coloured specs or a blindfold!"

**Karen Paull, Practice Manager,
Book-keeper and mum of teenage girls**

"This is an excellent book for anyone in transition. It's refreshing, light, balanced, well researched, manageable to read, full of 'light bulb' moments, encouraging and full of possibility."

Kathryn Wakefield,
HR consultant, RSA Group and world traveller

...

"Sarah's wonderfully easy, articulate style and illustrative anecdotes make *Choices* a great read and I found the practical exercises the most beneficial out of everything."

Nikki Lloyd,
Writer and fab mum of two

...

"A practical, easy to read and insightful book for anyone who has life choices to make. It challenges your hard wired thought process and helps take you on a journey to a new level."

Claire Blissitt, Commercial Development Director,
Kantar Worldpanel

ACKNOWLEDGMENTS

There are so many people that I need to thank that I'm not sure where to start. Having 'tried' to write a book over the last few years the difference this time has been in the commitment to it and knowledge of how to approach it.

For the commitment I want to thank my husband Marcus for being the best Dad in the world. Taking little Nick out every Saturday and most Mondays so that I could write has made this book possible. It also helped seeing the photos of the fun you were having together posted on Facebook as I was writing… smiles always help the creative process! I also want to thank Jules who was there when I wavered before booking onto the authors retreat with Mindy. Your straightforward approach of 'it's only three months of total focus' and 'it's been three months since I came to visit' put things into perspective for me. For knowledge I want to thank Mindy at the Book Midwife for being an amazing coach. You held me to account, set deadlines and provided invaluable insights on the art of writing. I'd also like to thank Nikki, a fellow writer, who one day during a walk on Hampstead Heath told me a home truth. Your challenge that I didn't need to go on a training course to learn to write was well-timed. It made me realise that it might be an excuse I was using to avoid getting started. It was the kick up the behind that I needed.

I also need to thank Martyn, Gina, Rachel, Claire, Karen, Kathryn, Steve, Nikki and Jane for taking the time to read my manuscript and give me feedback.

For inspiration and motivation I want to thank the amazing teachers, mentors, coaches and friends who include:

Jim McNeish – thank you for your wisdom, challenge and support and our walks around the lochs and lakes.

Dr Phil Holder – thanks for being such a creative mentor. You helped me build confidence exactly when I needed it.

Derek Osborn – thank you for showing me what was possible and the power of putting energy into relationships and your network.

Ian McDermott, Tim Gallwey, Tony Robbins – all for being great teachers.

Gertie Lane – thanks for being the kind of Mum that just gets on with things. For showing me first-hand the power of mind over matter and for continually 'fixing' yourself despite what the medics tell you.

… And a huge thank you to every single client, friend and team member that I have had the privilege to spend time with. Your stories, some of which may be in this book, are an inspiration. Seeing you make the sometimes difficult choices and flourishing has been inspirational and fulfilling. You are great teachers.

INTRODUCTION

As a Cornish maid who grew up on a council estate I've been fortunate enough to be sponsored by employers throughout my career to study with some amazing people. I know that not everyone is that lucky. So I hope in some way the sharing of my experiences can help and encourage you to make whatever choices you need to create the life that you want. My dream, and the intent behind writing this book, is to make accessible to as many people as possible the learnings and techniques that I have seen change people's lives for the better. I hope as you read you will discover things that you didn't know, be reminded of things that have worked well for you in the past and find that by looking at things from different perspectives you provide yourself with more choice.

Be all that you can be.
Know who you are and be true to yourself.
Do the best you can with what you have.

This book is your book, not mine. So use it however you like. Write on it, turn down pages, share it with others. Do whatever makes it useful for you, just don't not read it!

A friend who read the original manuscript for this book described it as a smorgasbord of yumminess. I loved her description because my intention when writing was to share stories, tools and ideas in a way that you could dip in and out as the fancy took you. Let's say it's more for snacking throughout the day than sitting and eating in large meals. Each chapter flows into the next and yet you do not need to begin on page 1 to get to understand what's on page 71. Each section is dynamically connected to the others and stands on its own at the same time. Of course if you want to you can start at the beginning and devour the whole lot in one sitting. If you do, I would advise allowing yourself moments to take a breather throughout. If you don't pause, you may not notice what's working for you or allow yourself the pleasure of 'smelling the roses' in the moment.

Throughout the book you will find personal stories from my life as well as stories from clients I've worked with. Within these stories I have changed the names of the individuals and not referenced specific organisations. This is to protect the confidentiality that is so important in coaching and personal development. I hope my use of personal references and stories brings the more technical or psychological aspects to life.

I hope you enjoy reading your book as much as I've enjoyed writing it.

Here's to creating and making choices we may never have dreamed possible.

CONTENTS

CHAPTER 3

CHAPTER 4

CHAPTER 5

EXERCISES INDEX

CHOICES

You always have choices and you know how to make them.

CHAPTER I

Take Responsibility – it's your life

The funny thing about life is that without choices there is no hope, and without taking responsibility for those choices there is no power. So responsibility seems core to having a great life and who wouldn't want that?

Decide what you want and say it out loud

Having to say 'I want' is something that I found impossible to say for years. Maybe it was the family modesty and Methodist upbringing that did it but 'I want never gets' is certainly something that I used to hear loud and clear in my own mind if not from others.

Deciding what you want is liberating. Being able to say it out loud inspiring. Being able to describe in specific detail exactly what you want is one of the most compelling and motivating things that you could possibly do in life. It'll be the difference that makes the difference.

Clarity = ease of deciding direction when you hit a fork in the road

Throughout your life there will have been many decision points and forks in the road so far. And for those of us who are living our lives rather than being hermits in caves then there will be many, many more to come. Every day we have decision points and choices to make. Do I have breakfast, and if I do then is it cereal or the sausage sandwich I really fancy? Shall I get up now or can I afford another 10 minutes in bed? Not that the lie-in is available in my household these days – you've got to love the energy of the two year old! These may seem like really shallow choices but they add up to a lifestyle. They can become habits and they impact on every aspect of our lives. A sausage sandwich on occasion is tasty but every morning may bring about an impact on your health that you may not have bargained for. The extra 10 minutes in bed if you take it could mean that when you do get up you feel fully ready for the day and much happier, or they could have been the 10 minutes you needed to make up for being stuck in traffic or your train running late so you end up sprinting into your first meeting of the day. For us to be able to make choices that are the best we can make, then we first need to know our direction of travel. A direction that takes us closer to our final destination. I'm not talking about writing things in stone, and yet research does show that if you write down a goal then you are significantly more likely to achieve it. The very act of writing goals down will make them more specific and clear for you. So I say let's grab a pen and get writing our wants for the future.

A favourite book of mine growing up was *Alice in Wonderland* and my favourite character the Cheshire Cat. He had a certain wisdom that has stuck with me over the years:

18

Alice – "Would you tell me please, which way I ought to go from here?"

Cheshire Cat – "That depends a good deal on where you want to get to."

Alice – "I don't much care where."

Cheshire Cat – "Then it doesn't matter which way you go."

Lewis Carroll, Alice in Wonderland

Although the Cheshire Cat was right in many ways, I believe there's a little more to it. It's one thing understanding that it's a good idea to know where you're headed, but how on earth do you choose and how do you recognise when you're coming up to a fork?

I'd say there are a few things to keep at the front of your mind:

1. Keep your eyes open – if you don't, how will you know where you are?

2. Don't travel too fast – you could miss some really significant turnings.

3. Choose a destination before you set off – it may not be an exact address but a general direction is useful.

4. Know yourself well enough to know what you'll need on the journey.

STORY

One of the biggest choices I've made, and one I'm happy to report that I love, is becoming self-employed in 2007. My fork in the road came much earlier than planned when I made the move from my corporate life. I had joined the HR team at B&Q as the Talent Manager. This was my first ever role in HR as I'd previously qualified as an auditor (studying at a military school – but that's a story for later) – and I'm eternally grateful to Mike my boss for taking the chance on me. The organisation was paying for me to re-qualify in numerous areas of psychology and personal development when I signed up for a 6 month programme in London. One of the 4-day modules was looking at the human behaviours that drive decision making, and as the style of the trainer was highly experiential we were testing the theories by creating our own visions for the future. As I began to consider the life that I wanted to create, what I wanted to look back on when I was 60, I realised that it wasn't having headed up some large corporate business or having built a reputation as the go-to person in the corporate world for thought leadership on HR and Learning and Development. Managing large teams was something I could do but as I reflected it wasn't something I took joy from. I was much more about helping individuals be the best they could be, and trusting that for the organisation if this was happening then the commercial benefits would come as the by-product not the driver. I loved the cultural work and the aspects of the role that impacted on people being able to be their best selves. The image I had in my mind was of a huge skip outside of the office building and as people arrived for work in the morning they would leave 70% of themselves in the skip… They'd come in and do a good job and then as they went home they'd collect themselves from the skip and become a whole person again. It became my mission to help people in the organisation to take their whole selves to work. Once I had clarity on this being my purpose and outcome, it came time to begin to plan how I could best go about working in that way. With clarity I also noticed that the skip full of 70%'s wasn't alone in my picture, it wasn't just one office building, it was all over the city, all over the globe. So this could only mean one thing – that I needed to be freelance to be in a position to influence as many people in as many organisations as possible.

The jump from Talent Manager in a large corporate in Southampton to a freelancer working for many organisations felt huge, but having it as a goal meant that when I hit my first fork in the road less than a year later, I could make my choice with more ease and certainty. The actual fork for me came in the form of a job offer in London of a role to head up Leadership Development in an organisation that – let's just say – was more in need of a turnaround than growing. I knew it would be a massive life-change for me and my husband – most people we knew were leaving London in their early 30s, not moving there. One fork was paved with comfort, our home by the water, certainty, long service, people that knew me and trusted in my skills, and the other was paved with uncertainty, excitement, the chance to work with a board that faced some real challenges, a move to one of the greatest cities in the world and an experience that would add to my dream of going freelance one day. It was a no-brainer. Emotional to say goodbye, but it just felt right. With the support of my personal career coach I was able to have the difficult conversation with my CEO to resign from the major project we had embarked on.

The next big fork in the road came a couple of years into my role in London – an opportunity to be able to engineer a redundancy. My plan to go self-employed wasn't meant to happen until 2010 and this was 2006... way too soon. But I had my eyes wide open and I noticed the chance to bring things to life sooner. Again, the logic was easy because I had the clarity of my future that I was creating, so the fork to leave was the way to go. This time my emotions were all over the place as it felt too soon. Again my wonderful coach asked me some brilliant questions that made my heart align with my head. He asked me to imagine what it would feel like walking into work on Monday morning having not requested redundancy; and then to imagine what it would feel like walking into work on Monday having made the request. The first question left me feeling heavy and sad and the latter one light, a little queasy but motivated. So with that sense of knowing, the logic of it being aligned to my longer term dreams and with the support of friends and family, I took the leap. Having been telling people of my plan for a few years, it felt really good to be able to call them and let them know I'd been true to my word and had the gumption to do it. Self-employment beckoned.

Now I realise as I tell my story that at the points where I hit the fork in the road I had my own version of the Cheshire Cat asking me the awkward and the helpful questions. Having a coach made all the difference – having a friend who was 'for me' and yet challenging speeded up my decision making and action taking. Here are a few questions that I've found useful at forks in the road when my Cheshire

Cat hasn't been around. I hope you find them useful. Try them now on any choice you're currently needing to make:

EXERCISE

....

Decide what you want – guiding questions

1. What do you want? What will it do for you?

2. How will you know when you've got it? What will you be seeing, hearing, feeling when you've got it? What will others be seeing, hearing and feeling when you've got it?

3. Can you start and maintain your outcome?

4. When, where and with whom do you want it? When, where and with whom do you not want it?

5. What do you get out of your current situation and behaviour that you might want to keep?

6. Is it worth the cost to you? Is it worth the time it's going to take? Is this outcome in keeping with your sense of identity?

....

Commitment is powerful

What are you committed to? It's not something I hear many people talking about. It's such a strong statement to say 'I am committed to x'. Maybe more marriages and teams would go from strength to strength and stay together if they spoke of their commitments rather than needs, goals and expectations. A commitment is more than desire, it's more than a goal and more than a responsibility. It has the heart of a lion and the head of a genius.

If all of you is in the game then you are committed. It's not something you can do from the side lines or the terraces. You have to be on the pitch to score a goal. Commitments create motivation. They determine how we act and react when times get tough.

One obvious commitment that we may choose to make in life is to get married. At the time I got married, in 1997, my then boyfriend (now husband) Marcus was working in the dairy industry with Devon farmers. I remember one evening meeting up with Marcus and him saying he'd been doing some research before we made our commitment to each other. Odd I thought, given that academia was certainly not an area that he was interested in, but I got curious anyway. He said he'd been out on his rounds with the farmers over the week checking in on their herds and had got to talking about marriage and asked them what makes for a marriage that lasts. At this point I got really interested because, as a Cornish girl that knows her fair share of farmers, I knew that most farmers manage a good 40/50 years wed… so if anyone knew the secret, they did. The answer that most consistently came back was, "Young people today just don't try!"

Commitment seems to have the quality of determination built in. It sends a signal to our brains that we are doing this come hell or high water. It speaks to the 'can do – will do' attitude rather than the 'which is easiest' approach.

EXERCISE

. . . .

Your commitments

Take some time just for you. Some time to take a breath and be honest with yourself. Some time to reflect and consider.

You may want to consider one aspect of your life like your career, or you may want to think about your whole life – once you've chosen, ask yourself these questions:

What are you committed to for your team?

What are you committed to for your organisation?

What are you committed to for your family?

What are you committed to for your relationship/ marriage?

What are you committed to for yourself?

You may find that some of these areas of life are easier to answer than others. If you do, then that can be an indicator of importance, neglect or loss. Whatever it may be, the first step is to notice. Then make a note so that as you progress through this book you may make some different choices in that area of your life.

With those I work with 1:1, I notice that it's common for women to find the 'what I'm committed to for me' question really tough. If this was true for you (whether you're a man or a woman), then maybe it's time to find and take care of yourself for a while. When was the last time you did something just because?

What are the things you love doing and when did you take the time last to do them?

Fear of failure can be debilitating

Failure is one of those words that never fails to create an emotional response. For some of us it takes us straight back to our school days and it can be a really visceral experience. The traffic light system that's used in a lot of organisations these days is set up in a way that plays to pushing the failure button for a lot of people. For those of you that haven't come across the system, it's really visual and can be incredibly helpful when used in a supportive and honest way where the culture of the organisation is one of focussing on outcomes not problems and blame. There are targets set and red, amber, or green applied depending on how you/the team/the organisation is doing against each, with red being off-track, amber being okay and green being on-track or achieved. So many organisations that I've worked with over the years end up with a false picture because they don't account for fear of failure when they set up the approach. For some, knowing the visual measure will be applied stops them from even trying, for others, they fake the chart and show the picture of a lovely green world when actually crimson is more accurate. This comes from fear and may not even be based on actual experience of anything bad happening if something is red or off-track.

There is a cultural memory that is held in teams and organisations that affects behaviour. It's hardwired in many ways for all mammals, something I realised when reading this story about some monkeys:

> An experiment placed five monkeys in a room with a banana tree in the centre. Whenever a monkey attempted to climb the tree to pick banana, a sprinkler system would spray all the monkeys with water until the monkey retreated from the tree. This experiment was repeated until all the monkeys learned to not approach the tree. The monkeys liked being dry more than they liked bananas.
>
> The next stage of the experiment involved replacing one of the monkeys with one who had never been sprayed with water. The new monkey soon started to approach the banana tree. However, before the sprayers started, the other monkeys jumped into action and beat the new monkey away from the banana tree. This was repeated every time until the new monkey learned not to approach the tree.
>
> The researchers continued to replace the original monkeys who were sprayed with water one by one with fresh monkeys. Eventually, none of the monkeys in the room had ever been sprayed with water for climbing the banana tree but the monkeys still continued to beat up any monkey for approaching it. None of them knew why they couldn't approach the banana tree. They just knew that it was off-limits.

A company's culture becomes intertwined with the 'standard best practices' that aren't questioned and never replaced.

Are there any 'banana tree' rules where you work?

For systems like the traffic lights, or any others where you can succeed or fail to make it work, you need to set a tone that failure is feedback. It informs our next choice and is therefore really useful. If Thomas Edison had given up after any of his first 1000 attempts to create the light bulb then we'd still be truly in the dark ages! Now I'm not saying in high risk situations that you wouldn't want to mitigate against failure. If I'm on an airplane then I only want the pilot to take off if she or he is sure that all systems are go and that there will be a successful take off, flight and landing. Learning by mistakes need not be life or death! This is about creating momentum. For most of us, if we fail at something in our careers or life it's not going to kill us or anyone else, but often the choices we are making can feel like they are about life or death. Some of us have an amazing skill when it comes to worrying and can't stop ourselves before we've even started.

STORY

This cultural norming and attitude to failure was brought to life for me whilst working with a global telecoms company over the last few years. It's given me real insights into different approaches to failure and how it impacts on business success, retention and recruitment of good people and, ultimately, achieving goals. Strategically, they were looking to diversify and wanted to take an entrepreneurial approach to building the business. Now it often worries me when I hear large corporate organisations talking about helping their people be more entrepreneurial, as it often means going on a course and not much more. It's great to learn the 'how to's' of being an entrepreneur, but if you are then back in the same large, open-plan offices of your organisation, where the hierarchy signs off ideas and you have to prove growth and be measured on a weekly/monthly/quarterly basis for reporting to the shareholders, then you are arguably on a hiding to nothing. What was great about the approach this client took was that they thought more broadly and modelled the successful approach of Silicon Valley and took the 'Fast Failure' business approach. The ethos was that for every 8/10 business ideas, the faster 8/9 failed, the quicker you could put resources and focus behind the 1 or 2 that took flight. Those in charge of the ideas that failed were as celebrated as those in charge of the ones that continued, as without all 10 you wouldn't find the gem. This bred behaviours where honesty abounded, leaders celebrated speed of testing and this engendered true reporting on how things were going as there were only positive consequences – failure was truly feedback.

What's your attitude to failure?

I notice three themes of approach when failure comes up. If I were giving them nicknames I'd call them the dabbler, the fighter and the master. Throughout my life I'd say I've been all three at different points with a bias towards dabbling in my 20s, fighting in my 20/30s and mastery in my 30/40s... although I know I still have a dabbler approach in my tool kit as I find it can be fun! So what the heck am I talking about? Well, let me introduce you to my three friends:

Let's think about sports to illustrate the dabbler approach. It's an approach that could be about careers, relationships, sports, life – anything really – but sports will certainly help clarify how to do it, so you can consider whether it's something you may do.

I take up golf, I've got a reasonable swing, I can get around the course without too much embarrassment, then I notice I don't seem to be getting any better so I take a lesson or two... and if anything I get worse. So I say to myself, "Ah well, I'm just not a golfer" and take up tennis. I hit the courts with my lovely new kit and I'm enjoying it, I can volley a little and I'm enjoying the game so I keep playing until I notice that I'm not improving, my game has plateaued so I say to myself, "Ah well, I'm not built for tennis, it's not my game". Next I try my hand at running. I'm building up my distances and am enjoying the outdoors until one day I can't seem to get beyond the once-around-the-park I've managed to achieve in 20 minutes.......so I say to myself, "I'm just not a jogger"..........next......

The Dabbler

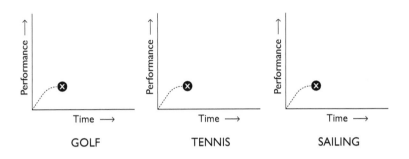

Now the fighter would take a very different approach to the dabbler. At the point where you hit the wall and plateau in skill your inner voice is saying something much more assertive to you. Taking the golf story from our dabbler friend... *I take up golf, I've got a reasonable swing, I can get around the course without too much embarrassment then I notice I don't seem to be getting any better so I take a lesson or two... and if anything I get worse. So I say to myself "I can do it, I must do it, what will people think if I don't do it... grrrrrr, get off your arse and practice more... go go go", or something along those lines as our inner voices all have different tones and levels of humour. The similarity will be that for the fighter, when you hit the moment of choice it's a struggle that you must fight your way through to get to the other side. You will have told yourself you are going to do something and irrespective of the pain or cost you will achieve it!*

The Fighter

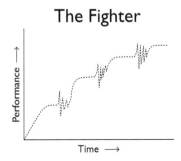

Last, but by no means least, is our master. For me this is the more mature of the bunch, energised and focussed but balanced with wisdom. The master, I believe, is who you are when you are operating at your best, especially when learning something new. So back to the golf story: *I take up golf, I've got a reasonable swing, I can get around the course without too much embarrassment, then I notice I don't seem to be getting any better so I take a lesson or two....and if anything I get worse. So I say to myself, "Ah, a plateau, I've been expecting you". I stay calm and call on my focus and motivation to continue to practice and work through the plateau because I know that I'll get to the next level if I stick with it. I understand that I'll improve for a while and then there'll be another moment of, "Ah, the next plateau, I've been expecting you too"... My awareness and acceptance that you must reach a plateau to improve means that when I hit the wall I get a sense of achievement, as I know I'm on track to mastery.*

The Master

> ## TIP:
>
> *Having met all three characters, consider which pattern you follow most frequently. Do you have different approaches in different areas of your life? Are they working for you, or would you like it to be different in some way?*

EXERCISE

The WorryBuster

If fear of failure is something that runs throughout your life, then let me introduce you to the WorryBuster! For any moment in your life where worry kicks in and it's not motivating you, in fact it may be holding you back, then this technique can get you moving again. Worry is an emotional response and, although sometimes illogical, it will always be well-intended. The most common purpose of worry that I notice when I'm working with clients is to keep you safe in some way. Be it protecting you from some imagined fate like reputational damage or saving you from being sacked, the worrying strategy wants to keep you safe... but sometimes it does just the opposite or can even stop you from getting something you really want through inaction.

The WorryBuster

The situation/ worry	The worst case scenario of what could happen	% chance of worst case happening	Need to mitigate against the risk H/M/L	Action
EXAMPLE: A customer complains to your boss about a service you have provided.	Your boss reacts badly, hauls you into the office and not only gives you a dressing down but fires you. You don't get a good reference, find it impossible to get a new job and can't pay your mortgage so are evicted from your home by the bank.	5%	Low	Write to customer offering apology for their feelings and copy in boss so that he/she sees that you have taken action to solve the issue before it escalates.

In essence what you are doing is:

Step 1 – Defining your worry clearly in writing.

Step 2 – Determining the worst possible outcome in writing.

Step 3 – Considering the likelihood of the worst case scenario happening and deciding whether to accept it or take action to mitigate against it.

Step 4 – Taking immediate action.

Attitude is everything

Every morning you have a choice to make as to which side of the bed you get out of (metaphorically speaking if not literally). That decision not only affects your day but impacts on anyone else that you come into contact with. There are moments in life where the idea of bouncing out of bed with a smile seems impossible... or even inappropriate. I can't imagine smiling as I got up on the day of my father-in-law's funeral. My family wouldn't have been impressed if I'd bounced around in an energetic, happy, upbeat way and it wouldn't have reflected how I was really feeling. Being true to your emotions and authentic is at the core of any choice. Attitude isn't about being 'happy' constantly, it's about focussing on your outcome and choosing the route to get there.

Live your life in the driving seat

Throughout your life you most likely will have met people who live their lives as the underdog or in a victim mode. You may even have spent time there yourself. Those times in your life where you hear or say things like, "You make me angry" or "When you do x, it makes me feel y". In these moments you will have chosen to be the passenger in your own life rather than in the driving seat. These are the times when you are 'at effect'. Taking the wheel and living your life where you choose in which direction you are going to head puts you firmly in the driving seat. These are the times when you are 'at cause'.

Being 'at cause' means that you choose to place yourself in the driving seat. You believe that you create things in your life and that means that you can change them no matter what the circumstance.

Being 'at effect' means that you believe and accept that others have control over your world and your feelings and you can do nothing to change it.

Now both of these things may be true. I'm not selling you the idea that others have no impact on us... and yet, if you were to allow yourself to imagine that you do create your own universe, what might then be true? If you do create your own universe then everything in it you have brought about. If you created it, then it does mean that you are more likely to come at problems looking to change them rather than just sitting back and taking them. You have the power to make the change.

In the work that I do I find that individuals can often be stuck at the point where they've given others the power in the situation by feeling that they have no choice to change things.

Many times I have had someone come and complain to me, "I have told him in so many different ways but he won't understand". As long as you have this attitude, you can't improve on your communication. You are not even acknowledging the fact that you have a problem. You have moved the problem to the recipient. This may make you feel good in the moment but it won't solve the problem.

What makes a massive difference to your effectiveness is if you shift your response to, "I have told him in so many different ways but he won't understand. I have to learn how to communicate in a way that he will get it". With this approach, you are taking responsibility for the communication, and you can start looking for new ways to communicate to get the result you want.

"The moment you take responsibility in your life, is the moment that you can change anything in your life."

Hal Elrod

STORY

I've been employed recently by a large charity to work with their Head of Policy and Brand, Jane. The objectives from the organisation's perspective were to support and challenge her to motivate her team to make the changes needed to begin working more commercially with their corporate partners. The HR Director had noticed that Jane had been becoming quieter and seemed subdued in comparison to her usual passionate manner. When I first met with Jane the initial thing I noticed was how she described the problem. She said, "The organisation makes me feel undervalued". For Jane, one of the things that has driven her to succeed and deliver has always been a sense of her own significance and that she was making a difference. So her statement was incredibly important to her and at the same time was keeping her stuck because 'the organisation' held all the cards and choices. By the end of the time we spent working together Jane came back to her belief that 'I make a real difference' and added to what she told herself – that 'I accept the cultural restraints in which I work, my boss is not an expressive man, there is always the door, and I can choose to leave and I can fulfil my creative needs outside of work'.

The key area that we explored to get started was looking at the beginning of her original statement – 'the organisation'. 'The organisation' is too abstract to be able to consider, so you need to ask who specifically is meant by 'the organisation'. In Jane's case it meant her boss John and the CEO Martin. By breaking it down to these two people Jane was able to consider the reality and step into their shoes for a bit. She realised that John is a contained and private person, and this allowed her to accept that this wasn't going to change no matter what she delivered at work. This acceptance meant that Jane was then able to explore what was important to her and was required so she would feel valued. She realised that her value came from being creative, and that in the past this had come from painting which she had stopped a few years ago. She also noticed that her focus had been on John and Martin's lack of response, and this had meant she wasn't noticing the positive emails and comments coming from other team members and the corporate clients about her work. By owning the relationship with John and asking his thoughts, and by broadening her view as to her metrics on 'doing a good job', Jane took control by changing her attitude to one of 'I have choice'.

EXERCISE

....

Time choices

Consider for a moment where you spend most of your time.

Are you living at cause and truly taking responsibility for what happens in your life? Or are you more at the effect of the world and feeling 'done to'?

Is your current way of living working for you?

What would be different for you if you were to live more at cause?

If you do want to make the change, then begin by breaking things down for yourself and by asking yourself – What do I want? What do I really want? If I could have one thing what would it be? How would I like to progress? What is my next step?

....

Born or learned – attitude can change

As a toddler, the way you will have learned will have been through cause and effect, by trial and error and by repetition. You will have dropped food from your highchair to test the reaction of your carer or to hear the noise as it hits the floor. You won't have known the word gravity but you were certainly using it to full effect. As we grow up, our way of learning at its core doesn't change – it just becomes more sophisticated. The significant experiences we have through life we store in our brains to refer to later. Significant doesn't have to be big or loud, it can be quiet and consistent. If you grew up in a household where your Mum was afraid of dogs, you will at best have no dogs in your life and at worst have frightened reactions to dogs as experiences to refer to. When you walk down the street or through the park, you may find yourself walking a different way or even having a fearful reaction as a result. This won't be because you had a bad experience personally but because someone you trusted taught you how to be when dogs were around. It can be as true in the workplace with certain types of people as it can be in the park with dogs. Who are the characters that push your buttons without even trying? Is it defensiveness around the office 'alpha male', or maybe irritation with the collaborative types? Noticing your habitual reactions and knowing that they are just that – habitual – makes a real difference, and gives you the choice to do something different.

When you are born, studies have shown that, through testing for specific chemicals, it is possible to measure whether you are a pessimist or an optimist by nature. So from this you might think, well, my attitude is set then… but it's not. Our neurology changes as we grow through experiences. Being pessimistic is something that I notice in Western society is valued and encouraged. To see the degree to which we can get things wrong and find pleasure in others' hardship seems to jump off every newsstand.

Now pessimism was an incredibly useful start back when we lived in a world with many physical dangers. If there was a chance that by stepping outside of your home you could be eaten by an animal or attacked in some way, then it would be a good thing to open the door expecting those things and being ready to react to protect yourself and your family. These days, though, we have few physical dangers. Most of our dangers are psychological, so our pessimistic views may be a little out of kilter and need some updating. For some the idea of being pessimistic is actually about being a realist. If I believe that we're born, we struggle and we die, then nothing will ever disappoint me. This may well be true, but if studies show that by being optimistic you are more likely to be happier, healthier and more successful, then why wouldn't you want some of that?

When I talk about optimism I'd like to be clear that I'm not talking about the 'happy happy ra ra brigade'. There's little more irritating than the person that's always sunshine and light, always cheery and giggly, and rarely aware of their impact on others. I'm not suggesting that we stand looking out on our metaphorical gardens of life and say 'there are no weeds'. Gardens, like life, have weeds in them. The alternative of standing looking into the garden and saying, "OMG, look at all those weeds, they're ugly and always keep coming back, will never go away and they take over the whole space", doesn't feel particularly motivating or fulfilling either. Maybe the attitude balance for best results is more of standing looking in the garden, seeing the weeds as well as the flowers, and pulling on your wellies, grabbing a trowel and going to dig up the weeds... or getting the local gardener around and picking some of the flowers to brighten up your home. None of the approaches are wrong, and I know which I'd prefer to live in and with.

If you agree that the optimistic life is for you too, then it'll be important to remember that a balanced positive attitude is all about seeing adversity as temporary and a one-off rather than as permanent and universal. It's about your 'explanatory style', which is your habitual way of interpreting the world around you, and adversity in particular. You can interpret events (good or bad) as being either one-off or universal, an example being failing your driving test the first time. Think of it as a one-off event that doesn't mean you'll always fail tests and exams. The other dimension to 'explanatory style' is temporary or permanent, so consider for example a broken leg. You could choose to think of the broken leg as temporary rather than something that will never heal. It's the same thinking patterns that affect how quickly you might bounce back after not getting the job you applied for, or finding that the promotion you had expected is now not going to happen. Whether at work or at home, the way you explain things to yourself makes all the difference.

I remember reading an article a few years back where a reporter and a psychologist visited a jail in the US to interview the son of a man who was currently on death row. The man had two sons, one who was in prison for violence-related crimes and the other who was a minister in the community church. They were interested in understanding how two brothers raised in the same family circumstances by the same violent father could take such different paths. As they reviewed their notes after the interviews, the reporter noticed one phrase that both sons had used in answer to the question, 'How did you end up where you are today (prison/church)?' They both answered, 'Well, what would you expect with a father like that!'

It's all in the attitude!

EXERCISE

....

Flexible Optimism, the ABCDE technique

Learning to be more optimistic can be much easier than you might think. One technique that I found quickly became habitual for me is the Seligman ABCDE for Flexible Optimism.

The ABCDE Technique

HAVE
- Adversity
- Beliefs
- Consequences
- Disputing
- Energising

CHANGES

Ref. Martin Seligman

Let's say I'm on my way to a job interview and the new dress I bought for the meeting turns out to be one that creases a lot (the <u>adversity</u>). I have no time to be able to rectify the situation so I have to attend the interview in my crumpled state.

The <u>belief</u> I have at this point is that the interview panel will take one look at me and think I couldn't care less about my appearance, that I'm not organised enough or that I'm not respectful enough of their organisation or them to make an effort (the belief).

The <u>consequence</u> of this belief would be my being in a defeated state before I've even entered the room. Am I likely to get the job in that frame of mind? No!

Now it's time to <u>dispute</u> the belief, the way of thinking about the adversity. Consider what else might be true. So maybe it could be a talking point, a way of building rapport with the panel in the waiting area before the interview. Maybe they will have had a similar wardrobe failure in the past. Maybe the linen-like quality of the material will remind them of their last holiday and put them in a positive frame of mind. Many other things might be true, or none of them may be, the point being that as soon as you begin to consider alternative outcomes your <u>energy</u> level increases. By becoming more energised in the way you affect the consequences of the adversity you are therefore more likely to get to a positive outcome.

With a great attitude you can do anything

If after reading 'you can do anything' you have a picture of a liberally thinking, over enthusiastic, X factor contestant's parent in mind, then please do think again. You're in a space of expanding opportunities by thinking widely rather than by shutting yourself down... not deluding yourself or others into considering yourself an expert or the next Whitney Houston! All of you who have worked or are working in sales are likely to have had the Henry Ford quote shared with you on many a training course, and for those of you who've missed out on what the incredibly industrious chap said, it was, "If you believe you can, or you believe you can't – you're right". To take a single black motor car and add in the idea of mass production to fulfil the passion to make the innovation available to 'the common man' takes true belief. It changed the world!

To achieve anything takes flexibility of approach and 100% responsibility. There is something very powerful in accepting ownership of your own life and outcomes.

STORY

You can take your inspiration and example from a diverse number of places, from Victor Frankl, the Second World War concentration camp survivor, Terry Waite who was taken hostage in the Middle East, or even my Great Aunt Helen.

Most of us will luckily never have a life event that's as dark or extreme as Victor Frankl or Terry Waite, and yet we can learn so much from their stories in terms of how attitude affects our life. Victor Frankl believed he had more choice than his captors. He knew he could respond to whatever they did to him in a way of his choosing. He accepted he had no control over what they did and yet he knew he had a choice of how to respond. Even on the darkest days this man, who was not treated as a human being, chose to respond to each prison guard as if they were an individual with their own hopes and fears, likes and dislikes. His decision and attitude in such dire circumstances helped him to survive to become an inspiring writer and teacher. Terry Waite, a hostage in the Middle East, chose to respond by writing a book in his head about his experiences as they unfolded.

Now let's consider Great Aunt Helen, not as dramatic a story and yet possibly more relatable. When we were kids visiting her in her Cornish bungalow, we used to gather in the kitchen because washing dishes with Auntie was so much fun. As we helped out, many family tales were shared and wisdom dispensed. I realise now that Auntie probably didn't love the washing up. It was the infectious nature she brought to the task that made it fun for all of us. This is something that has certainly stuck with me when facing what otherwise would be a mundane task and has helped motivate teams over the years.

Knowledge comes second

It's said that we now live in the knowledge age and I guess that's true if you're comparing us to the age of manufacturing, the industrial age or when agriculture was the life force of the economy. Travelling around the globe does show you that our view of which age we are living in does somewhat depend on the country you were born in and even your economic status.

Here in the Western world the knowledge age is definitely where we are. It's around us all the time, everywhere. In fact some of us pay lots of money to get away from it and I certainly have worked with senior executives on disciplining themselves about accessing it. The call of the BlackBerry... that little blue light flashing, or the ping of your iPhone saying that you're wanted, you're needed, someone has something to say to you... it's compelling and addictive for some. Gone are the days of endless, and sometimes fun, debates and persuasive arguments with friends about which is the longest river, what the name of the boys' school by the millennium bridge is or who won the world cup in 1970. Now we can know the answer within a few seconds. The generation growing up today may never feel the need to set foot in a library and certainly not to do research in the way I remember it. Learning the Dewey decimal system, I'm guessing, is probably no longer on the teaching plan in schools.

Today learning is more accessible than ever before and can be obtained quickly and creatively. Having knowledge and being a life-long learner is a joy. It is also a choice, both in terms of for how long you learn and how you use the knowledge once you have it. Having knowledge for some can become their way of being powerful within organisations. Ever heard someone say, "Knowledge is power"? Not a healthy attitude to how to use knowledge in my experience, but one I've certainly come across in my working life. I notice that those who hold onto knowledge create divisions and fear-based, non-learning environments. It's something I find a little odd in that, for me, if I love knowledge and acquiring new learning, why would I not want to share it? Power and a need for security are two common reasons I've come across. Often the need for power comes from a place of fear too. The fear that, "If I don't know enough or more than others then what's my value – I'll be let go". It can also be driven from a fear of failure, of getting it wrong or being seen as not on top of things. This fear has often been a core reason for behaviours like micro management or being seen as lacking strategic thinking when I work with leaders in organisations. Tackle the fear and you let go of the behaviour – you change the attitude.

You'll have had moments in your life and career where, looking back, particular individuals have had a momentous impact on the paths and choices you took. At the time some may have seemed small or even insignificant, others you may have known were to be life-changing. All will have set you in a certain direction.

STORY

When I think about knowledge and attitude, the best example that I've experienced was at a turning point in my career. I'd decided that the world of finance and certainly being an auditor wasn't a good match for my strengths, and I had already managed to make a move within the global organisation I was employed by into the commercial function as the Procedures Manager (sounds about as exciting as you might imagine). It was low risk for the Head of Commercial to take me on as the job was aligned with my previous financial and structured way of operating. It opened up the world of relationships and negotiation as I was, in essence, employed to translate for the solicitors, buyers and producers and get them talking the same language. After 18 months I knew that I wanted to spend more of my time with people, helping them develop and by doing so, make a difference to both them and the business. The role of Talent Manager was posted internally and at first glance I thought, 'Nah, there's no way the HR team is going to take someone into that level of role without any HR experience'... and then I thought of good old Henry Ford and his, "You believe you can, believe you can't" quote. He was sitting alongside motivational speaker and author Tony Robbins who was shouting, "Feel the fear and do it anyway" and my old teacher Mr Robinson saying, You don't know until you try"... As an imaginary influencing team, they were strong! So I went for it and got in touch with the recruiting manager Mike. To this day I owe Mike a huge debt of gratitude because, had he not held the belief that knowledge comes second to attitude, I would never have got my first break into the world of personal development that I love. His feedback to me after the interview was that a fast learner who is willing and up for the challenge can get up to speed in the time he needed them to fulfil the role. Mike was a real teacher that day, truly believing in individual talent and giving someone (me) the space to grow and fulfil my potential. Now, with over 5,000 hours of coaching and development under my belt, I've held that belief and reference experience as one of the core principles that guide me and has meant that many other people's lives have changed too as a result. Thanks Mike. ☺

Acceptance can be empowering

There are times in our lives and careers where we find ourselves in conflict of some sort. It could be with another person or you could be fighting with yourself. Either way, we can sometimes miss the fact that for each of these battles we have a choice whether to engage or not. We are the only mammal on the planet that has been gifted with the ability to choose our response when something happens, rather than reacting immediately with fight, flight or freeze. True 'response – ability' or the ability to respond.

The only person you can change is you

Although in life it can be tempting, frustrating and sometimes seem like the only option to attempt to change what someone else is doing – accepting that 'the only person you can change is you' can save a huge amount of time, effort, blood, sweat and tears! For any change to take place there are two key elements that need to be present, being willing and being able.

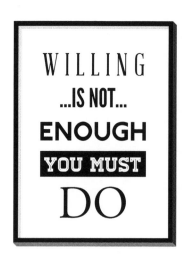

WILLING
...IS NOT...
ENOUGH
YOU MUST
DO

So if someone else is a block to you achieving your outcomes, then they need to be both willing and able to change. Without the desire then nothing will happen. A far more effective approach can be to change yourself, your own behaviour. I've seen and experienced for myself the power and magic that can happen when we make a change. Whether it's down to mirror neurons, the human desire to fit in, or our inbuilt copying-to-learn habits from childhood I don't know, but the old saying of 'smile and the world smiles with you' seems to hold true.

STORY

I've been working with a client, Jo, in the media sector who was up for promotion to a senior director role in her global organisation. Her challenge was that she was being held in her current role because her boss, Adam, had a serious illness, and the executive team were mitigating the risk for the organisation by having her stay on the team in case Adam had to leave for an extended period of treatment. It was known that the likelihood was that within 18 months Adam would choose to retire but, in the meantime, there was a business to run. Working with Jo, we began to uncover that the frustration she was feeling about being stuck was leaking out and potentially damaging her reputation. We also realised that the 'promise' that Adam's role would be hers in the future may have been well-intended but was possibly more about avoiding conflict in the present moment. There was a second role opportunity that Jo had negotiated as a possibility for secondment that would take her off-track in terms of promotion but aid her in maintaining equilibrium in the short-term to repair her reputation. So, Jo was in the position of considering what she wanted. Was she to hang on in the current stressful situation waiting to see what happened with Adam, or should she push for the secondment that would keep her sane but take her off-track or just leave? The key moment came for Jo when she broke out of her cycle of 'it's not fair – I should get the promotion now and they should deal with the underperformance of Adam' and accepted that the board member in the decision-making chair wasn't going to change his conflict-averse style. Once Jo accepted this, she became much more able to see clearly and, without the knots-in-stomach emotion, she was able to make a plan that was true to her own needs as well as being fair to the business. Acceptance created space to make a better decision, a better choice.

EXERCISE

The meta mirror – perceptual positions

Think of either a great relationship where communication is amazing or one where communication is just not working. In either instance make sure it's one that you would like to understand more and/or change.

Now, either in your mind's eye, or in reality, get prepared to sit in some different seats to see things from differing perspectives.

When you are in seat 2, if you are doing the exercise physically moving, then it can help immensely to take on the physiology of the person you are thinking of. If they slouch, you slouch. If they sit with folded arms, you sit with folded arms. Whatever they typically do then you copy and do your version of it.

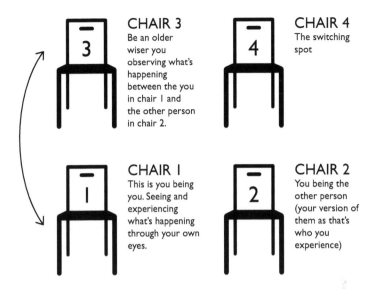

CHAIR 3
Be an older wiser you observing what's happening between the you in chair 1 and the other person in chair 2.

CHAIR 4
The switching spot

CHAIR 1
This is you being you. Seeing and experiencing what's happening through your own eyes.

CHAIR 2
You being the other person (your version of them as that's who you experience)

Steps:

1. Sit in chair 1 looking at chair 2. Ask yourself, "What am I experiencing?" Notice how you feel in your body as well as other sensations. What are you thinking and feeling?

2. Move

3. Sit in chair 2 being your version of the other person. Sit as they would sit. Look back at yourself sitting in chair 1. As before ask yourself, "What am I experiencing?" Notice how you feel in your body as well as other sensations. What are you thinking and feeling?

4. Move

5. Sit in chair 3 being an older wiser you. Look at what is happening in chairs 1 and 2. Ask yourself, "How do you respond to that you over there?", "What do you want to say to her/him?"

6. Go to chair 4. Visualise switching the you in chair 3 with the you in chair 1.

7. Go to chair 1, and being you looking at chair 2, ask yourself, "How is this different now?"

8. Go to chair 2, and looking at you in chair 1, ask yourself, "How is this different now?"

9. Go to chair 1 – come back to being you.

A high percentage of people find that this technique works after one repetition and others find that repeating the process a number of times gains greater clarity. This is often the case where the relationship is long-standing or the emotions are running high. It's fine and really helpful if you repeat it a number of times once 3 and 1 are switched.

....

Acceptance and 'giving up' are not the same thing

By accepting something you are empowering yourself with more choices; this is not being weak. You are taking a stand by owning where things have got to and doing something about it. A conscious choice to accept a behaviour, a situation or a reality means that you can then choose how best to use your energy rather than have the situation running you and taking all your energy to manage it.

STORY

....

I remember a time in my corporate days when I would get eaten up with anger and frustration. The trigger for my frustrated reaction was when my boss the Human Resource Director would take his red pen to any board presentation I had lovingly prepared. My face probably told of my feelings, but I used every ounce of energy I had in those situations to hold things inside myself and react rationally and in a politically astute way (shouting at your boss or crying through frustration may be a little career-limiting!). I got to a point that whenever I knew I was needed to present on a given topic I'd start dreading it even before I started. (Not the best state to be clear or creative, I can tell you.) So I took a step back and had a little laugh at the state I'd allow myself to get into, which at that moment helped a little but wouldn't solve the repetitive nature of my problem. I wanted to be able to relax and continue to do my best work. Acceptance and understanding were key to my making a sustainable change. I realised that for my boss there was a reason he took his red pen to my work and it was nothing to do with the quality of what I had produced (most of the time anyway). His reasons were about him and his need to feel useful. He was a driven man who needed to add value, and since taking his seat on the board he had found that the value he was adding was no longer tangible – you couldn't see it directly because it was through his thinking or his team that he made a difference. So I was offering him a gift whenever he reviewed a presentation – the gift of feeling that he was making a tangible difference. Something people could see and that he would experience when I gave the presentation at the board or team meetings.

Once I'd realised that the red pen behaviour wasn't to do with me I was able to not only accept it as one of my boss's quirks but that I was actually helping him feel valued by providing an opportunity. I didn't have to change anything, I simply needed to frame my thinking in a different way and our relationship changed overnight. I was much more relaxed around him and we were both able to do a more effective job... and for me it took much less energy.

Choose your battles wisely

In any given day where we interact with others there are a multitude of opportunities to change things, fight for our viewpoints or offer our help. It might be with the other parents in the school playground, at home with your partner or at work with your colleagues. Have you ever experienced what I would describe as the 'red mist'? That moment when something is triggered in you that means you zoom in on something or someone 100% and with great energy express your views. The level of focus that comes with the mist can be powerful in terms of winning the battle or getting what you want in the moment. Sometimes though we can miss the collateral damage that occurs, the damage we may do to relationships on the way or the more literal physiological or psychological impact in the moment.

Our emotions are hardwired to our physiology. Our wiring may have subtle differences because we are all unique and yet our patterns may be more similar than we realise. The next time you feel a negative emotion notice your vision. Negative emotions like anger come with focus or focal vision. Our pupils get smaller and we lose the ability to see things on the periphery. It's something that back in the days when we needed to hunt for our food was incredibly useful. We would have the rush of adrenaline when the kill was in sight and raise our weapon, our vision would become more focussed and be set on the target and we would then throw the spear or shoot the arrow. Today though, a trip to Tesco doesn't require the same focus but our brains when we find ourselves in an adrenaline-inducing situation produce the same pattern and reaction. Not having your peripheral vision available to you can be dangerous, so it's good to know that you have a choice and that you can use your body, your physiology, to impact on your emotional state and manage the red mist. The need for peripheral vision is perfectly shown in the police training for high-speed driving. If you're called to an emergency and have your blue lights flashing then the likelihood is that adrenaline will be kicking in, and if your vision became intensely focussed then you would no longer notice the people on the pavements or the cars pulling out from driveways. You would be totally focussed on what was immediately ahead of you. One way of mimicking the police training is to imagine a tennis ball on each corner of the exterior of your vehicle and to maintain focus on them. This simple act means that speed can be achieved whilst maintaining awareness. Try it next time you drive – it can help manage road-rage, keep you within the speed limit and it's fun. Win-win!

EXERCISE

....

The Presenter State

If you would like to practice using your physiology to manage your emotional reaction in times when you are under pressure, the presenter state is an easy exercise that you can use. It may be that you practice it specifically for the next time you have to stand up and speak at work or it may be that you use it to maintain calm throughout the day you're with your children; either way practice, practice, practice and you'll notice a change.

Get a piece of A4 paper and draw a big black dot on it. Now stick it on the wall around 4 metres away directly in front of you and at around eye level. Now stand looking towards the dot, feet flat on the ground a shoulder width apart, take a deep breath and stare at the spot. Notice at this point what you can see in your peripheral vision. Now lift your hands to either side of your head and wiggle your fingers. Continue looking at the spot and move your hands, fingers still wiggling, back in a straight line heading behind you slowly. Notice how your field of vision widens and anything else that may move in your peripheral vision you notice really quickly.

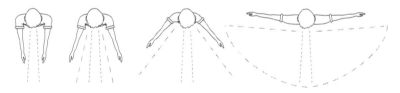

With practice you will develop the ability to switch into peripheral vision/presenter state at the moment when you might need it and the great news is that you'll do it without having to carry a dot with you.

....

Take control of what you can then let it go

Serenity prayer

God grant me the serenity to accept the things I cannot change; courage to change the things I can; and wisdom to know the difference.

Living one day at a time; Enjoying one moment at a time; Accepting hardships as the pathway to peace; Taking, as He did, this sinful world as it is, not as I would have it; Trusting that He will make all things right if I surrender to His Will; That I may be reasonably happy in this life and supremely happy with Him Forever in the next. Amen.

For this to hold true you don't need to be religious or have any form of spiritual calling. Regular Sunday attendance is not required... it's a metaphor and for me, you can take out all references to God or Him and the essence remains true.

Accept the things you cannot change, have the courage to change the things you can and be wise enough to know the difference.

When life gets hectic, or you find yourself under pressure, the temptation is to revert to your preferred and habitual way of being. You may not take the time to notice that you have choices or that you can stand still for even a second to notice what the best action might be.

STORY

....

When I first started working as a freelancer I was lucky enough to have the opportunity to join the team at a global, international pharmaceutical company at their London offices. I was called in to be part of their work creating corporate athletes. The part of the programme that we delivered was around team resilience and looked, amongst other things, at how as individuals in the team you handled and reacted to pressure. With one particular team I was warned before running the session that there was a high probability that a fair number of them would focus on the location of the offices when we got onto the topic of pressure at work. Anyone who has ever driven past or visited the offices will notice the sheer scale of the building. It's a fantastic facility with an in-house gym, a number of restaurants, a convenience store – basically a high street inside the building! So the chances of the company moving location anytime soon is very slim. At which point I re-evaluated my approach to the session to make sure that the team got the most from the time rather than spending hours talking about something that was never going to be possible. That's where the following exercise helped immensely. Rather than explain the theory, here's the structure and I encourage you to do it for yourself. Grab a pen and paper:

EXERCISE

....

The pressures categorisation

1. Make a list of all the pressures you are under at the moment. They might include things like: job insecurity; family and childcare responsibilities; study and keeping up to date at home; budget constraints and limited resources; the increasing pace of work; the need for fast decisions; significant fast and continuous change; learning a new skill at work; economic demands to work more effectively and efficiently; two careers per family; elderly parents to care for...not an exhaustive list for sure.

2. Now you've made your list let's get categorising to help make sense of your pressures. Populate the box below with the pressures you've listed. Add in any more that come to mind as you write.

3. Notice any patterns or areas that are more prevalent for you? Is one box fuller than the others?

4. Decide what's next. For those outside of your control – how might you accept them or respond to them in a different way? For those inside your control – what might you want to change? For those internal pressures – what's driving them? Consider working through them with a coach/mentor to reframe them.

	Under your control – you could reduce/eliminate them	Outside your control – you could change your response
Pressures at work:		
Pressures outside work:		
Your internal pressures:		

CHAPTER 2

Your inner team is running the show

Inside each of us are many different players – our inner team. It's a rare individual that is exactly the same in every environment with every type of person. In fact you could even argue that life would get pretty boring if we were. Throughout your life so far you'll have met most of your inner team, you just may not have thought of them in this way before. You may have thought about your personality and how you are in different environments or with different people, but just not considered those personality traits as something you have any control over, or as a team you can call upon consciously.

We all have multi-faceted natures

A common time when the inner team becomes clear is when we say or are feeling, "On one hand I want to do x and on the other I want to do y." So for you, it may be that the healthy, fitness-freak part is set on going to the gym and the social, party-loving part wants to go to the impromptu drinks after work with your colleagues. If you were one dimensional, then life would be rather flat in every sense. Knowing who in the inner team you've got available, all the different sides of your personality, gives you greater choice and makes your behaviour more conscious.

First know who's in your team

If you were tasked with pulling together the best team to deliver on a particular project, the first thing you're going to need to know is who you've got to choose from. Then you'll want to find out more about them, their strengths and weaknesses, their motivations, their needs and wants. To be able to get the right mix and be sure to get the best from your team you'd want to get to know them well. You'd want to understand who works well together or where the potential conflict points are. This is exactly the same with our inner team – it's just we've never been sent on a course to learn about managing our personalities and facets! It's an area that sadly only seems to get looked at when things go wrong. When people are in crisis or are having mental health issues, our capacity to be resourceful is examined, but rarely is it considered when we're getting by or doing things well. Where inner struggles exist you'll often find self-sabotage (even in seemingly successful people).

STORY

··

A friend of mine, Anne, asked for some help a few years ago because she'd been struggling with making a decision about whether to leave the music industry. Through her 20's and early 30's she'd loved her role finding new talent, but now as she came to her mid/late 30's the 3am finishes weren't quite the fun they used to be. Her professional self knew it was time for a change but the playful minx part of her wouldn't let go of the lifestyle. When we got to talking about what was really going on for Anne, she started to realise that for her the inner struggle was about security versus fun. Both the parts of Anne wanted her to be happy and safe – the professional in her wanted to take a step in her career towards financial security that would keep her comfortable in later years but the minx wanted her to be happy in the moment and enjoy the time she had now. If we hadn't got to talking about her inner team, we may not have got to the point of understanding that we could work with both parts to reach a compromise. Anne's solution was to take a role still within the industry but working with new creative ways of using existing materials. No more late nights, the seniority to keep the salary and the fun of still playing in the music space.

EXERCISE

....

Who's on your team?

Have fun with this exercise. Relax and enjoy it. The last time I explored sub-personalities I was in Scotland with a great friend and psychologist Jim, and I walked around the loch to clear my mind as I pondered the questions he'd posed about my inner team. Maybe you'll find it useful to find a space that does the same for you. It could be the local park, by the ocean, in your garden or a quiet space at work. Wherever it is, make certain to relax and enjoy the exploration:

- Think of sub-personalities that first come to mind and write them down. To help, think of how you show up in different scenarios:

  - At home/work/outside

  - When you are in conflict with yourself – what parts are in conflict?

  - When you are with certain people groups – members of your family, certain friends, boss, team, etc.

  - Common pervasive emotional states you fall into – worrying, manic, childish, serious, fussy, caring, charming, etc.

- For each one – recall being in that sub-personality. Remember doing what you were doing, what you were saying, what you were feeling at that time. Ask the sub personality the following questions in order to get clearer on its nature and make it more distinct.

- What three words best describe your personality?

- What do you look like?

- How old are you?

- In what situations do you get called up?

- What do you need/want?

- What would be a descriptive nickname for you?

Whether you've captured your sub-personalities in a list or in a more visually creative way, you now have a greater knowledge of who's on your team. You can pair them up, choose specific characters for certain situations or simply just know they are there. Whatever you now choose to do, you have a greater self-awareness and that means more choices.

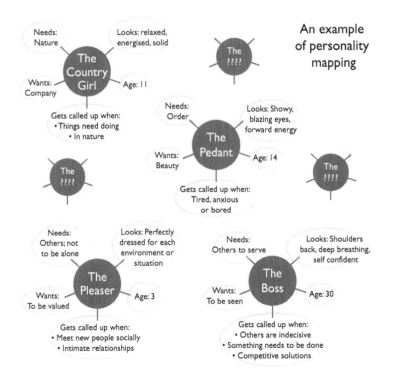

An example of personality mapping

Getting to know your dark side

Without dark there's no light. Without contrast things blend to a point of being invisible. Emotions and behaviours such as anger and the act of being angry so often get labelled as bad or negative. Now, in some situations I may be inclined to agree, but it's circumstantial. You're walking home from work or having a quiet walk around your local park and someone decides to mug you. They push you to the ground and steal your bag or wallet. In this instance I would say that being angry is healthy, it's wholly appropriate. Whereas if someone fails to return your 'good morning', then the same level of anger may be considered a little extreme!

Working with sub-personalities and your inner team comes with the challenge that to get a true sense of everyone in your team you need to be honest with yourself. You need to notice and get to know the 'nasty' or 'dark' characters. Without them in the team then tough moments in life or handling difficult people can become impossible. Our drive can go out of life if we fail to embrace our whole selves. Or we may find that the dark side gets louder or more cunning at finding ways to express and let itself be known.

One dimensional living is boring

Imagine for a moment your favourite meal. Take yourself back to when you were last enjoying it. Remember the environment, who you were with, the smell of it, the look of it on the plate, the textures as you take your first bite… Now imagine that for the next 40 years that's the only experience you'll have. The only meal for the next four decades! I'm willing to bet that some variety would be your choice with food. That on a summer's day you're less likely to want a hearty stew and on that cold winter's evening an ice cream may well not hit the mark. So if variety and making choices that fit the environmental factors are considerations with food, then why not consider them when you think about your personality? Taking the same old version of you into every situation, although predictable and consistent, may not fit the bill for achieving what you want.

You have opportunities every day to show your different sides. Whether it's your adventurous side as you explore the local woodland or attempt a new approach at work, or it's your sensible side kicking in as you make a decision on which car to buy or who to hire to join your team, each situation and role calls for a different set of perspectives. You are still being you, that authentic person that is at the core of everything, you are simply showing a different side. I find it interesting that for many of the people I have worked with, and indeed among my family and friends, the only part of life that they may have set goals around and thought about how they are perceived, is at work. Taking time to think about their different roles in life and what they want to achieve hasn't even been a consideration. This is often where a pinch point can arise, a conflict of time and energy, because, for example, you may feel that you're not being the best mum you can be because you're working full-time but you've never really thought about what your internal measures of what being a good mum are. So you are setting yourself up for a guilt trip and failure before you even start.

EXERCISE

....

Roles and responsibilities success mapping

To be clearer about what success looks like for you, and to get a clearer view of the opportunities you have you need to be able to tap into more of yourself. To do this you may want to begin to think about it in terms of roles:

1. Review your roles and responsibilities.

   Think about the different roles you have in life. Don't worry about getting it perfect... just list whatever comes to mind. Some examples of roles include:

   – Wife/husband/significant other

   – Religious/spiritual group member

   – Parent/family member

   – Sports club member

   – Manager/Team member

   – Carer

   – Community/school volunteer

   – Home manager

   Once you have identified your roles, record them in an easily accessible place.

2. Set goals for each role or responsibility. What do you want to achieve? What kind of manager/friend/parent do you want to be?

Consider the following questions:

- What is the most important thing I could do in each role in the next week to have the greatest positive impact?

- What is truly most important versus urgent?

Based on your answer to these questions, think about one or two goals that can be accomplished in the next week for each of your roles. Record them in your diary on Sunday or Monday as goals for the week.

You may want to think longer-term too and consider your long term outcomes.

3. Plan weekly... schedule your priorities

Plan weekly instead of daily. Schedule in your diary a time during which you will accomplish your goals (step 2) in each area of your life for the week. You should schedule other responsibilities and activities only after scheduling your priorities. Remember to leave some gaps in your schedule to allow for flexibility and new opportunities.

4. Exercise integrity in the moment of choice

On a daily basis, revisit your goals for the week to avoid getting side-tracked. As new opportunities arise, weigh their importance against the goals you have set and make your decisions based on the level of importance.

5. Evaluate your performance

Making sure you notice first what's gone well, evaluate your performance at the end of the week. Did you meet your goals in each area of your life? What challenges did you encounter in meeting your goals? In making decisions, did you keep your priorities in mind? How can you use your experiences this week to be more effective, both personally and professionally, next week?

Role	Goal	Activity	Schedule
1.*e.g. friend*	*To feel connected*	*Facebook updates x4, phone call or text weekly*	*Facebook ad hoc whilst travelling. Diarise call on a Thursday evening.*
2.			
3			
4			
5			
6			

The example I give above may seem a little over the top, however it's a real one that I set myself a few years ago when I noticed that because my closest friends are hundreds of miles away or on different continents, time would run away and I might not speak to them or know what was going on in their lives for months. In a busy life, time seems to go slowly by the day but faster by the month. Be honest with yourself when setting your activities about the medium you use and whether it fits your style. Consider, for instance, are you naturally organised and disciplined or more spontaneous? Choose a method that plays to your strengths and you'll succeed more easily.

Playing to strengths gets results

It has always confounded me as to why, in the Western world, we feel the need to train ourselves to be good all-rounders. Our schooling system is set up to make sure that, irrespective of natural talents, you study science, languages and maths, do sports and something creative. This approach means that all too often you may have experienced the sense of frustration of failing because you were having to do something that you weren't built for. It's a bit like being forced to write with your right hand if you are left-handed, and it isn't that long ago that in the UK children's knuckles were hit with a ruler if they used their left hand to write. My older brother, who was at school in the 1970s, experienced this, and to this day his handwriting looks uncomfortable. He can write in a way that does the job of communication but it's neither beautiful nor fun to do because he was trained to go against his strength.

Where you focus your energy goes

Our brains take in information and stimulus through our eyes, ears, and touch. We are multi-sensory beings. Once the stimulus is occurring, our bodies and minds react. Your unconscious mind is in charge, it decides on the best reaction in the moment. Because of the integrated way that our mind and body operates this means that wherever our attention goes our unconscious tunes in and reacts – whether you meant to or not! So if you spend your time focussing in on the bit of your job (or your life for that matter) that you're not great at then that's where your mind and body puts energy. All of your energy – a disproportionate amount usually. You may well find that you get better at the thing you weren't great at, but at what cost? This is not what I imagine you'd want for yourself?

STORY

Before sex addiction and his bad behaviour came to the media's attention, you may remember that Tiger Woods was famous for being the world's best golfer. For me his story is a perfect example of how playing to strengths rather than focussing on weaknesses truly is the difference that makes the difference when it comes to results. When he was a very young golfer his original coach directed most of his attention to his bunker shots. Now Tiger at this point in his career was something like 164 in the world when it came to his bunker shots and in the top 10 for his drive. It seems logical to focus on and practice the area where he was weakest and yet it was only making incremental improvements to his game. At this point his coach changed and so did the approach to getting the trophies and closer to the green jacket. This new regime was about focussing on strengths, playing to natural talents. So most of the time on the course was spent practicing his drive because this was where he was already great – top 10 remember – the idea being that the more accurate he was with the drive the less time he would spend in the bunker anyway! Now the coach wasn't so naïve as to think that in the heat of competition mistakes couldn't happen. He got Tiger to practice his bunker shots to a point where he could get himself out of them if needed, but he spent the majority of the time focussing on the areas of his game where the true talent could shine. By 21, Tiger was the youngest man to ever win the US Masters and a succession of wins followed over the years.

EXERCISE

···

Know and own your strengths

To be able to focus your energy on your strengths you first need to recognise what they are. Because our strengths come so naturally, we can often take them for granted or not realise that they're something that not everyone can do. An old colleague of mine in my days in finance used to be able to scan over the business accounts and in a heartbeat be able to tell the commercial story: where the highs and lows were, the themes and areas that needed attention. Watching him do it was a joy, it was as if the paper had contours and he could see the bumps in the road. I could clearly see it as a strength because I couldn't do it, but for him it was just something he did. He'd say things to me like, "Can't everyone do the same thing? It's so easy," without hearing my answer, "No they can't, it's a real talent".

Step 1. Make a note of those things you already know to be strengths. It may be the things you've had others comment on in the past like my colleague in the story above.

Step 2. Consider what those closest to you would say if they were describing you to a stranger. What insights might that give you into what they notice you do most and best?

Step 3. Ask them. Decide whose opinion you value, let them know why you're asking and get them to choose the three words that they believe best describe you.

Step 4. Believe them and say thank you!

···

Be wary of your Achilles heel

I remember clearly the day when I realised that most weaknesses or Achilles heels are overused strengths. It was in 2002 and I was working with my CEO on a diversity project to understand and improve the number of females in our boardroom and senior management positions. My boss at the time was reviewing the research and results I was beginning to come up with. I'd asked him to give me the male view on the best way to describe the current organisational traits that impacted on the recruitment and internal promotion of women. We were categorising the traits when it leapt off the page – things like competitiveness, which was one of our commercial advantages in the market, had become so overused that internal competition had kicked in, the old dog-eat-dog mentality. This meant that we were, as an organisation, killing creativity and collaboration. The ones that were getting promoted were those that were the most demonstrative in having a competitive edge and this often seemed to come with success at all costs even if it was to the detriment of the long-term view or to other members of the team.

In organisational life there is a pattern I notice when it comes to what behavioural style is rewarded. There are times when you are rewarded for having an all-round balanced skillset and attitude, as well as times when it's rewarded to be seen to have a spike in your strengths. When you first enter the job world you get ahead by showing you are good at 'stuff' (the plural of 'it').

You're encouraged to be a good all-rounder. You then get to the stage of promotion to the junior manager level where you have a team to manage. At this point you need to be showing a more pronounced skillset in your chosen area of work and you need to be a good people manager. Then it's into middle management which takes you back to needing to gather skills across your field and demonstrate being a good all-rounder again. At this stage you are managing managers who have their own spikes of expertise. If you want to get into senior management, it's back to needing a spike, to demonstrating what you stand for, what you are best at, your strengths as a leader.

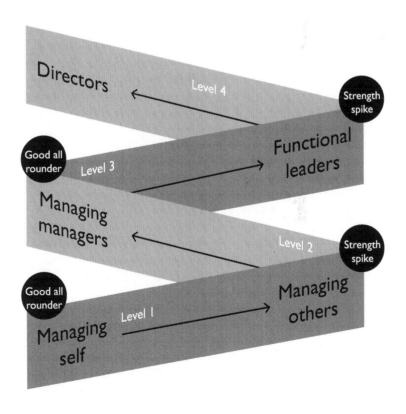

STORY

....

This knowledge helped reframe the situation that a client of mine found himself in. The client, James, was Head of the Commercial Department in a large UK retailer. He had been on the succession plans as the future Commercial Director for around 4 years. Next to his name on the succession plan it always stated that he was 12 months off being ready for promotion. He was 12 months off promotion every year for 4 years. It doesn't seem to add up, does it? This had got really frustrating for James, and when he had conversations with the CEO and the HR Director they talked about gravitas but weren't able to get specific enough for James to feel able to make changes so that the next time there was an opportunity to take the promotion he would be ready now rather than in 12 months.

As we worked together it became clear that there were a couple of blocks in James's way:

1. He was demonstrating being a good all-rounder when what the CEO needed to see to be able to welcome him around the board table, was his spike. What he stood for. What he would bring to the senior team table. It was a given that he could do his job. What was needed was that something special that we all bring and is clear for others to see.

2. James held a belief that directors were somehow super beings, incredibly driven and clever and that he wasn't one of them. Now directors are often driven and clever, but super beings? We needed to challenge James's belief that he didn't fit around the table because as long as he didn't believe he was a director then why would his CEO?

The Boardroom is full of 'uneducated' people

Like James, some of you may look at the boardroom or those at the top of your organisation and feel in their shadow, or you may even be sitting around the table with your peers and thinking, 'Who am I to be sitting here?' What I'm really interested in is how many of us, like James, see seniority as something that only comes to the most educated, those really clever people who must be almost super human. If you believe it, what impact is that having on the choices you make?

Having been privileged to work with many board members over recent years I can say with confidence that they are normal folks like you and me. They have insecurities, flaws and they don't always have the answers. Do they have energy and are they driven and bright? – YES. Does that mean that they all got firsts from Oxford or Cambridge University? NO. When first entering the executive coaching arena I believed that to be in the top seats in any organisation you would have to be a university graduate and well educated at an early age. A preconceived idea and one that meant I would often sit in the boardroom waiting for my client and smile to myself thinking 'if only they knew'. My belief was reinforced by my own choices as a teenager about education (as a romantic Cornish lass I dropped out of my A levels, because I fell in love and followed my heart). Over time my belief was challenged and experience has proved that it's about as real as the tooth fairy.

The more senior the people I worked with the more I noticed three themes arising regularly:

1. Most of the people I was working with, like me, had not formally finished schooling in their youth, they'd returned to it to gain professional qualifications in later life.

2. A number of them had similar thoughts to me around 'if only they knew – what would they think' – the fraud syndrome, and,

3. The way of thinking and the approach to business was more energetic, flexible and creative than structured and clinical – getting to the outcome was the key, not the route to getting there.

> *Studies show that over 66% of CEOs are appointed internally and 53% did not have a university education.*

One of the most common prompts for people to work with me is when they hit the block, the supposed glass ceiling. It might be when someone has been at a senior level knocking on the ceiling for a while but never quite managed to get through. It might be as a support to help fast-track those with high potential in the organisation. With both, a common trait that often needs work is around educational beliefs for those who didn't attend university. Some may have latterly attained professional qualifications or even degrees as adults but something in them still seems to fight against themselves when it comes to thoughts on education. At its worst it can be passive/aggressive in nature and manifest itself in a pushy and obsessively driven way. These behaviours may have worked well in the early stages of their career. Up to a certain point in their organisation it could have been seen as youthful drive and determination, but then it stops and it can be confusing that it no longer gets applauded. Imagine that you are one of up to 12 executive board members and you are recruiting for a peer. Are you more likely to want to welcome the pushy one or the one that has a relaxed air of gravitas?

STORY

....

This played out when I was working with Sarah from an international aid agency as part of my role as career coach for their talent programme. It became clear that she was a very accomplished woman. She had every skill and experience necessary to be welcomed into the director's suite but it just wasn't happening for her. The organisation had told her she had what it takes, and yet over recent years she had been overlooked for appointments and was getting frustrated and distrustful of the organisation's ethics. Over the period we worked together we were able to pinpoint the root causes of this, including her emotional reaction to 'educated' people. She had an internal anger about how she had failed in her teenage years and been rejected as a result, and even though she had since become highly qualified in her field she harboured those grievances at a deep unconscious level. To release the emotions we used the technique below to work at a somatic level. The problem was being held in her body not her head, so Sarah could have continued to gain more knowledge, thinking it might fill the void or solve the problem, but she'd have been looking in the wrong area as the problem was elsewhere.

EXERCISE

....

Decoding your negative beliefs

If there is something in your life that you would like to feel differently about then this is the tool for you. It works first time with 99% of people who want change, and for the other 1% it may take a couple of goes, and it'll work for you too – as long as you truly want the change.

With Sarah, her belief was so unconscious that we needed to get to a physiological understanding of how she had coded the belief in her brain rather than to reason with it. As an intelligent woman she fully understood what was happening and what needed to change but felt unable to let go of it... as if it was hardwired and there were no other options.

Your brain is incredibly good at filing information and has a way of referencing information using visual, auditory and felt elements. This enables you to know immediately if something is good, bad or indifferent, as well as giving you a sense as to whether something is true, untrue or questionable.

Below is a checklist of each of these categories for you to be able to begin to map out your own coding and then be able to change it if you choose. With the checklist in front of you, think of a belief that you currently hold that you wish you did not have. It could be that people who work part-time never get promoted, that once you're over 40 you're no longer attractive, that being dyslexic means that you don't fit in the corporate world, that not having a degree makes you stupid... the list of possibilities is endless. Consider one that you hold for yourself at the moment.

Now that you have in mind the belief that you would like to be different, ask yourself the following questions:

1. As you think of the belief do you have a picture?

2. Using column 1 on your checklist, elicit the details, e.g. is it colour or black and white?

3. Next, think of something in the past that you held as true that is no longer true for you. For example, the belief that you are 10 years old or that Father Christmas is real. As you think about that old belief do you have a picture? Notice where it is located and make sure this picture is separate from the earlier belief so that you can focus on it clearly.

4. Using column 2 on your checklist, elicit the details, e.g. what is the pitch of any sound?

5. Now change the details of the unwanted belief to that of the one that is no longer true.

6. Test it – ask yourself, "Now what do I believe about that old belief?"

7. Next, to reinforce and create a new belief consider a belief that is absolutely true for you. For example, a belief that the sun will come up tomorrow or that it's good to breathe. As you think about that belief, do you have a picture?

8. Using column 3 on your checklist, elicit the details, e.g. is the picture steady?

9. Ask yourself, what would you like to believe instead

of the old belief you used to have? As you think about that belief, do you have a picture?

10. Change the details of the new belief to those of the belief that is absolutely true for you.

11. Test it – ask yourself, "Now, what do I believe?"

Picture detail	1	2	3
Visual	Do you have a picture?		
Black & white or colour			
Near or far			
Size of picture			
Location			
Focussed or unfocussed			
Movie or still			
Amount of contrast (high/medium/low)			
3D or flat			
Framed or panoramic			
Bright or dim			
Angle viewed from			
Are you in the picture or watching?			
Auditory	Are there any sounds?		
Location			
Direction			
Loud or soft			

Tonality			
Pitch			
Duration			
Fast or slow			
Pauses			
Timbre			
Felt/ Kinaesthetic	Are there any feelings?		
Location			
Size			
Shape			
Intensity			
Moving or still			
Vibration			
Pressure			
Temperature			
Weight			

Your schooling may be holding you back

Having a structured way of thinking can be incredibly useful and, some might say, is the foundation of a civilised society, but too much can quell creativity. The formulaic way of working that is learned throughout schooling can hold you back from being your best. Nothing ever improved without some aspect changing and that requires flexibility. Otherwise things would stay exactly the same as before, no better or worse, just the same.

As children we are socialised into the norms of the place we live, the parents we grow up with and the school we go to. These things offer security for us as we grow. Holding on to the structures as we get older though, can become rigid and linear in nature. This in itself isn't such a bad thing, however in the world today what strikes me is that the only constant is change, and fast change at that. If change is the new constant then being rigid and linear is unlikely to create success either in business terms or life more broadly.

STORY

One Sales Director that I worked with was a fascinating example of how our beliefs around education can have a huge impact on our career, life choices and success. Steve had been working in his current organisation for around five years, he'd outstripped the other group companies in terms of sales and had grown his business by over 20% year-on-year. His energy was impressive and his ability in building relationships with key customers (mostly large organisations) was something to model as it was so natural.

With this proven commercial track record you would have thought he would have been a key candidate for the next Managing Director role in the organisation. His ambition and numbers fitted the bill but he had been overlooked for the last MD post. Through exploration and interviewing a number of his peers it began to become clear that the very drive that made him successful commercially was holding him back internally in terms of reputation. Steve held a belief that because of his lack of formal education he had to prove himself to be 'good enough' constantly. Now whilst it's true that your reputation is important and those on the promotion panel would need to have a clear idea of what you bring to the table as a leader, you can overdo it. A sprinkle of pepper on your pasta can be nice but the whole peppermill can be hard to take. Once we had spent time understanding where his beliefs about his education came from, Steve was able to relax. Simply knowing some of the statistics and hearing stories about other 'uneducated' leaders allowed him to bring his best to the fore without forcing anything.

I'm really pleased to say that Steve got back in touch with me recently to say that he hadn't got to the MD level in the organisation he was in when we worked together, but he was now an MD. He had taken his new, relaxed confidence and landed the role of MD at one of the organisations that had previously been a client, and he'd made a life style change in a much broader sense. He and his family had moved back home to the West country. It seems his chilled nature allowed for more than just promotion!

Be conscious of your environment

One of the keys to great communication, and therefore to getting to your outcomes when working with others, is being able to respond to feedback. Feedback doesn't need to be someone offering you their opinion. It can be much less overt. Often the most useful feedback loops are as subtle as the atmosphere. Anyone who has ever walked into a room where there has just been an altercation knows what is meant by atmosphere. It's the thing we can't touch or see but we can certainly feel whether it's positive or negative – it's real.

Sending in the wrong team member can be catastrophic

Having a highly tuned environmental radar is one of the most useful skills in life in my opinion. No matter how clever or skilled you might be at something, if you can't read your audience or pick up on the vibe to judge timing then you are likely to fall flat. It's something that allows you to be able to decide on your approach and on which members of your inner team are most likely to succeed. Sending the joker in at a funeral probably isn't the best approach, and yet at the wake he/she may well be exactly what's needed to lighten the mood and remember the life not the death of the loved one. Similarly, at work your competitive side partnered with your inner ethics champion may be the perfect team for winning that contract but may not be best placed at your performance appraisal.

STORY

....

Setting yourself and others up to succeed can be the difference between getting to your outcome and falling short. In my last corporate role where I headed up Leadership Development and Talent Management for a FTSE 250 organisation, part of my role was to bring in experts in their field to work with us. Now because my reputation depended on bringing in good people, I would expend a lot of energy checking out potential partners and, before organising for them to meet the CEO, James, or other board members, I would often experience their work first hand. There was one company that I was keen for us to use because I had spent six months training with them and as a result had personally made changes that paid dividends, both in my career and at home. Let's call the company ACME Training and the guys I invited in Frank and David. It's useful to know that both Frank and David are recognised in their area of specialism as being at the top of their game. They are both renowned speakers, have worked internationally for many years and are highly qualified. The pitch meeting for the partnering contract on a cultural change programme should have been a breeze... but the inner team choices that David made were an instant mismatch to James's style, and to say they clashed may be an understatement. David took the approach of the softly spoken and highly intelligent psychotherapist and expert (his inner guru), which in a more academically driven environment with a more introverted character might well have worked. James is a classic entrepreneurial type, a self-professed barrow boy and someone who values fast paced intelligence with an experiential edge (he needed David's warrior to show up). The pitch failed, and as a result James then questioned the whole idea of needing any cultural change to impact on business results. My lesson from the impact was that even those who can deliver at the highest level and are trained experts in psychology need hand-holding at times, and that if they have their environmental radar switched off they are likely to take the wrong team members and approach. You live and learn, and this for me was a turning point from where I was able to recognise the power of coaching and how it can, when used in day-to-day conversation, make a real difference to your outcome. If I had coached David rather than briefing him, he would have been better able to be flexible in the moment and change his approach to be able to influence James and, in so doing, help those in the business be better able to create high performing teams that delivered results.

Reading the room is a powerful skill

Being able to read the environment is the foundation for being able to decide your approach and that includes which of your inner team are most useful in the situation. The great news is that it's an area that can be developed, should you choose to. With practice all of our senses can be heightened and we then become better able to read any room. Anyone who has had the opportunity to experience Heston Blumenthal's culinary magic at the Fat Duck will have come away knowing that the more senses are involved in an experience, the more fully you are in it. By taking away your sight, your senses of smell and taste are heightened. By adding in the sound of the sea when eating a fish dish we are accessing the memories of being at the seaside and that affects how we feel about what we are eating.

Our senses can be described under five heading descriptors: Visual (sight), Auditory (hearing), Kinaesthetic (touch/feelings), Gustatory (taste) and Olfactory (smell).

The most powerful of these is olfactory as the nerve endings in our noses are the only ones in our entire bodies that are exposed to the outside world. This means that a smell generates a full body reaction and our brains release more signals, chemicals responses and memories as a result. So the perfume or aftershave you choose may have more of an impact on an everyday basis than you had realised – so choose wisely!

You will have experienced the impact of the olfactory sense daily but maybe never realised its impact on your mood or where you have noticed that you may not be choosing to use it to your advantage. If the smell of fresh bread makes you feel comforted and warm, then when you are feeling pressure and you want to change it, a trip to the local bakery may be all that's needed. Or if fresh-cut freesias remind you of someone you love (for me it's my Mum), then make sure to have them by your desk or in your hotel room if you're away from home for a spell to keep your unconscious mind feeling connected to that person.

In the same way as having a bias in terms of which hand we choose to write with, we will have a sensory bias too. What I find really interesting at a global level is that 70% of us have a visual bias – "I'll believe it when I see it!" It's one of the reasons that television is so much more popular and powerful in terms of media than, say, the radio. A bigger proportion of the world's population find the visual sense the easiest means by which to understand the world and live in it.

STORY

In a work context, probably the best way that I've seen this knowledge used was by Disney when they were working on *The Lion, the Witch and the Wardrobe*. I was visiting their offices in Hammersmith, London to offer some support to a friend of mine who worked in their people development team. Meeting rooms, as I find in most large organisations, seem to be in great demand with very little space available, so we opted to call in a favour and use the project team room for the up-coming movie. As we walked through the typical open-plan, relatively un-colourful space, the first thing I noticed at the end of the corridor was the sound of music playing quietly, entrancing music that was like a lute or magical instrument being played. Next I saw that where you would expect an office door to be there were old-fashioned wooden wardrobe doors! As Louise and I walked towards them and reached out and opened the door, the music stopped and a gust of freezing cold air came through. Inside the room there was the usual desk with chairs but they were standing on a bed of artificial snow, and the coat rack had a number of faux fur coats hanging on it. You couldn't be in the room without feeling like you were in Narnia! A brilliantly creative way to make sure that every team member for every meeting on the film was totally engaged in the creativity and story.

TIP:

Next time you hold a meeting choose your environment based on the emotional state you want the attendees to be in. Go to the zoo if you want them to think family friendly or have childlike curiosity, the science museum if you want a sense of history with an inventive 'anything is possible' feel, or even decorate the space you have to reflect the type of thinking and behaviour you want. Use the visual and auditory aspects to create a kinaesthetic (felt) reaction.

EXERCISE

....

Building your awareness

If building your ability to tune in and read a room would be useful, here are a couple of games that you can play that exercise the muscles needed to grow this skill:

Step 1 – find a friend or two to play the game with.

Step 2 – decide whether you want to work on your visual or your auditory ability.

Step 3 – start to play

Game 1

If you spend a lot of time on the phone or listening to others you may want to develop your auditory acuity – get 5 coins of different types, say a 1p, 2p, 5p, 10p and £1. First, calibrate your hearing by having one of you drop the coins whilst you watch. This way you can match the sound of the drop with the right coin. Next, close your eyes or turn around so you can no longer see. One of you drops the coins and those with their eyes closed have to name the coins dropped. The challenge is to get it right a minimum of three times in a row.

Game 2

If your work requires you to notice details or, if in life you would like to be more aware of your surroundings, then you may want to develop your visual acuity – one of you thinks of someone they really like and someone they really don't like. Once you've decided on the two people then the other person gets to calibrate their senses. So first think of the person you really like, allowing the other person to notice what happens visually to you. It might be that your colour changes slightly or your eyes soften, your breathing may quicken or you may relax your shoulders... There are a million subtle tell-tale signs you'll see once you really start paying attention. Then you think of the person you don't like and the other player calibrates their senses again. Now the game or test begins. You think about either the person you like or don't like without telling the player watching which it is. Their aim using only the visual 'tells' is to accurately say which one you are thinking of a minimum of three times in a row. Then switch so you each have a turn. It's good to remember here that the aim is to be natural and not to trick the person so that it's difficult – simply think of the people and that's it, your body does the rest. What's consistently amazing with this game is that even though you know it's not 'real', your body has unconscious tells that others pick up on.

External or internal referencing – which is best?

As a human being you are born with preferences. Your environment and upbringing have an influence on them, but at your core they still exist. A little like being left or right handed, you're adaptable, and if you couldn't use your preferred hand for some reason, such as injury, then you would switch and learn to use your less preferred one, but as soon as you were able you'd switch back again because it's more natural. One of the preferences you will have is about the way you reference things. Referencing is an odd word, I know, and you may be thinking, what the heck is she on about, so let me give some examples to hopefully create some clarity.

External referencing – For some of you, you'll have an external reference point for making sense of your world. You'll look for signs and indicators outside of yourself to know that you are on the right track. You may need feedback and praise to feel motivated and sure that you are doing a good job, and you will likely be aware of what is going on around you all the time. This is my preference, and in my last office-based role I had to move my desk because I was positioned within both sight and earshot of the doors onto the floor from the lifts. This meant that every time they opened I couldn't not look up and it had a huge impact on the amount of work I was able to do and my concentration.

Internal referencing – For some of you, you'll have an internal reference point for filtering your world. You'll often feel like you 'just know' and are guided by an internal knowing and check in that doesn't require others' input to know you're on track. You may find that this is a result of knowing who you are, of having a strong identity, which means that decision making comes easily for you. It may also mean that in team or group environments you may not build connections or rapport with others easily. An old boss of mine is internally referenced and at work the upside was that she was great at holding true to what she believed to be the right direction for the team. The downside was that she rarely noticed without prompting when she was losing the support of others, and the team was becoming demotivated and going off track.

STORY

A few years ago I was chatting to a fellow coach at a conference and he had just finished working with one of the world's top airlines on a contract looking at their recruitment of flight crew. The process, I believe, was truly innovative and used knowledge of internal and external referencing as a way of identifying those who may have a natural bias for customer care. On interview days the recruiting managers would observe the candidates in the reception area, looking to see their reaction to a series of activities and events that occurred. By observing at this early stage, before the candidate turned on the interview style, they were able to notice the referencing bias. Some would stay with their head in a book or reading other materials (internal reference indicator), whilst others would be doing the head bob, looking up every time something happened in the environment (external reference indicator). As part of the whole process, this was used as a way of knowing the likelihood of individuals being highly attuned to customer requests and the visual signs that they needed assistance. I wish that some of my local restaurants used this method when recruiting waiters. Sometimes I might be almost jumping from my chair waving and they don't notice. Totally internally referenced!

The really useful thing about knowing your preference isn't to change it, it's to choose jobs and environments that work well with your bias. Being internally referenced as a doctor I imagine is a really good thing, whereas if you're a criminal lawyer it may be easier to read the jury if you're externally referenced. It can also help with understanding how to motivate yourself and others. Externally referenced people look to the external world for feedback whereas internal referencing may see it as an interruption and unnecessary.

Know where the door is

Your level of awareness of your environment and surroundings has an impact on how you feel. It's important to remember that in any work situation there is always choice. The choices aren't always easy or inviting but they exist. The one that is often forgotten at work is that you can choose to leave – to go through the door. Resigning is an option, one that means you always have choice. Now I'm not suggesting that our choices don't come with consequences, so it may be that for you financially you need a regular income and to give it up without anything to go to might mean insolvency or losing your home. I imagine for a lot of us this has some truth to it, but at the same time it doesn't mean that the door has disappeared. It may mean that when you find yourself in a position that you don't want to be in, you need a staged approach to changing it. Knowing the door is there in those times can be what keeps you sane.

Knowing where the door is can help manage stress levels if you are someone who stands out. Standing out from the crowd and being very different from those around you can have its benefits, but it can also be tiring. If you are the only poppy in a field of daisies you are very visible every moment of every day.

STORY

When I decided to qualify as an auditor I looked to the professional body to research which schools had the highest pass rates for each of the papers, those which did the three-year programme in a shorter time as I was working full-time and wanted to push through fast, and those which ran face-to-face lessons coupled with distance learning. The one that hit all these criteria was the School of Finance and Management at Winchester military base in Worthy Down. I was accepted onto the programme and will never forget my first accountancy lecture. I was definitely the only poppy in the daisy field! The tutor was called Spike and wore full soldier fatigues, and everyone else in the room either worked for the government or the military. Being the only corporate civilian was an interesting experience, and although it took a while for me to settle in, I loved being the different one. Unfortunately this love of being different couldn't be maintained. It worked for me in the learning environment maybe because it was in short bursts throughout the year, but in my day job I just didn't fit. My style was too extroverted and people-focussed to work in the finance team that I was based with. After much soul searching and the odd heated debate it became clear that for me my best option was the door. The key moment was in accepting that the culture within the profession wasn't a natural fit for my personality and that acceptance and letting go was the most effective plan.

EXERCISE

....

Making your move

Self-coach questions if you find yourself stuck in the wrong field:

1. Do I like to be unique and stand out from the crowd or am I more traditional by nature?

2. In my life/work situation does it help or hinder to be seen as different?

3. Which environments do I feel most at home in and why?

Make a list of what's important to you in relation to a decision that you are currently considering. Maybe it's a new job search or you're moving home, buying a new car or going on holiday. Whatever it is, having the following personal checklist can help gain clarity to make your choices.

Must haves	Negotiables	Must nots

Consider everything from the financials, e.g. salary package, through to travel or commuting, culture or vibe.

....

Your surroundings impact on your behaviour

Imagine you're walking down a dark wood-panelled hallway surrounded by book cases full of large bound journals… How much might you feel like laughing or chatting? Now imagine you're entering a building that has an open space with many different colourful types of seating areas, some formal with tables and some more like your local Starbucks, there's music playing and people quietly chatting around you… How much more relaxed and open do you feel in either situation? Whether you're more relaxed and able to be yourself in formal or informal surroundings will depend on your life experiences and your personal style. Neither is right or wrong, and yet not knowing where you feel able to be at your best makes a huge difference to your quality of life.

From Victorian times colour has been actively used in our homes to generate emotions that are appropriate for the use of the room – oxblood red for dining rooms as it was believed to aid digestion, or lilac in bedrooms for its calming effect. It's not just the colour that has an impact, it's the content of rooms and the flow of how you are able to move around a space.

Today the arts of interior design and colour therapy are commonly used in homes and offices throughout the world and generate ever growing sums of money in our economy. It's forecast that by 2015 the interior design industry will be worth US$40 billion!

STORY

··

The impact of surroundings on the subconscious and mood
played out whilst I was working with a corporate client on
a cultural change programme. I was visiting their London
headquarters to meet with team members for interviews to
better understand the unwritten rules in the business, i.e.
the 'this is the way we do things around here' unspoken
way of operating. One common theme that emerged
from the interviews was that some of the sense of a lack
of respect that the teams reported seemed to be connected
to timekeeping. It was the norm for people to turn up to
meetings at least 10/15 minutes late, and often scheduled
1:1 reviews and work appraisals were de-prioritised and
cancelled at the last minute because of the run over in
timings. As I sat talking through my observations and
findings with the sponsor for the project, I looked up to
check the time and realised that the meeting room we were
in had no clock. After checking further it became apparent
that none of the meeting spaces in the seven-storey building
had clocks. In psychological terms this would likely be
sending an unconscious message to employees that time
was not important, and in practical terms no one would
be visually reminded of the time during meetings, meaning
that the likelihood of running over-time was heightened.
As a test and as a symbolic act for change, we decided
to put clocks in all the meeting rooms by the following
Monday and then observe and monitor any change in
behaviour. The plan was to not announce the change and
the clocks were fitted after the offices closed so there was
no disruption that would bring the change to individuals'
attention. After a month I re-interviewed some of the team

members I'd spoken to earlier under the guise of a review, and without asking a direct question about time, a theme emerged that respect was building in the teams. Managers must have really listened to the feedback because 1:1's were now happening and things ran to schedule more often than not, with people turning up for meetings on time.

One simple change can make the world of difference!

TIP:

Next time you want to make a change start by considering how the physical environment might help or hinder new behaviour.

CHAPTER 3

The truth, the whole truth and nothing but the truth

Honesty is often high on the list of things that are important to people but what does honesty really mean? It's one of those words, those nominalisations, that aren't really real. You can't go and buy some at the shops or put it in a wheelbarrow. It's a feeling, something that has a set of different criteria depending on the person. What's honest for one person may seem cruel or overly direct to another. Anyone that's ever been asked by a friend, "How do I look?" will have had the experience of the degrees of honesty that are available in the moment. Does saying, "You look great" when they don't, and then suggesting there may be a need for a jacket on top of the dress, mean that you are lying and being a bad friend? Does your pretence that it could get cold when really you are suggesting the jacket to cover the hideous pattern on the dress mean you're being dishonest, or are you being considerate of someone's feelings? It's all subjective and based on our own beliefs and criteria around what is appropriate in any given circumstance.

Honesty begins at home – inside you, with yourself

If you're not honest with yourself, you could easily be living someone else's dream. Or at best you may be 'should-ing' to yourself. By 'should-ing' I mean that inner voice that says to you, 'You should go to the gym more,' or, 'You should be ambitious and become a senior manager by 35'. I'd love to start a campaign to have the word 'should' banished from the English language. To date I've not managed to find a sentence that it can be used in that makes you feel good or motivated in any way!

Early influencers have a big impact

As children we learn by role modelling, by copying those around us. We take in what we see being done and we make a meaning of it that becomes our truth. What we are told becomes secondary – seeing is believing. Anyone who has had a parent or carer who said 'Do as I say not as I do' will know that. The chances are you may have listened and obeyed when you were really small, but by the time you were able to pick your path then you most likely did what was done rather than said.

As parents you might know that it's good to all eat around the table and have conversation from an early age with our children. You may even say to them that this is the truth... but if you then do something different, like most days grabbing breakfast as you run out the door to work and choosing to eat in front of the television after a hard day at work, then the message that you are giving is totally different from the words you've used. Which would you believe and what would you copy?

STORY

....

As a child I grew up in a Methodist household in West Cornwall where my Dad was a telecoms engineer for the General Post Office and my Mum was a stay-at-home mum who then worked part-time when I went to school. Now, neither of my parents ever said to me things like, 'Get a proper job and we'll be proud', or 'Any illness can be overcome without doctors', or, 'When you have children make sure you keep working or you'll lose your identity'. If they had I probably would have argued the points as they sound pretty extreme and inflexible. But despite no-one ever saying them, I did take on each of these beliefs. I noticed what happened in the world around me, what those I loved and those who had major influence on me like teachers did, and I made meaning of it like any child will do. It's how as human beings we become the amazing complex characters we are. Some of the meanings I made have been incredibly helpful and still are today, and yet others took me down a path that I really wasn't suited to. The 'get a proper job' inner voice took me into the world of banking and finance – not somewhere a creative soul really gets to flourish. I wouldn't change my experiences, as having them has meant I am better able to relate to and work with those in that world, and having a sound financial training does mean that you are a more credible business person. If I had been going down that path knowingly though, I might have chosen different timeframes and/or qualifications. Conscious choice would have had an impact in a positive sense.

EXERCISE

....

Key influencers and meanings

Explore the key influencers you had growing up and the meanings you made, in order to notice whether you are running an old pattern of behaviour habitually. Develop your conscious choice and identify areas you may want to change.

Person	Significant thing I saw/heard/felt from them	Meaning I made of it	Does this belief still serve you today? Is it useful?
Examples: Mum	Seeing her go from arthritic claw-handed to able to knit and use her hands freely	You can mend yourself – mind over matter is real	Still current and useful so one to keep
Teacher	Seeing them shout at kids for not getting the right answer	You must avoid getting things wrong at all costs	Not useful any more. More useful to believe that failure is only feedback and helps you improve.

1. List all those people you consider were key in your life as a child, e.g. teachers, parents, carers, siblings, friends, doctor/dentist.

2. Consider and write down any meaning or belief that came from each of these areas.

3. Is it working for you today?

As an alternative approach for those of you who aren't fans of structure and box grids, a frame that I find useful when considering beliefs is to write down:

The truth is…

and I believe…

Do this about key areas of your life and see what emerges.

....

Build a life YOU want

You may be choosing to read this book because you are at a point in life where you're considering where you've got to, the impact of the choices you have made so far and whether you want to make a change going forward. You may be reaching that moment, usually around a significant birthday when we reflect on what we've done with our lives so far. Or you may have had the experience of losing someone important to you which has reminded you of your mortality. Some of you may have experienced that 'wake-up call' moment, others may be simply curious about what is possible. Either way, making a choice about the life you want to build, the one you want to look back on from your rocking chair in old age can only be a good thing.

When considering the life you want to create, I notice that there are two common preferences in terms of approach. One is incremental and opportunistic. It starts from today and builds up to what then is possible. The other is to start with the end in mind. Create a vision of what you want in the future and then work backwards to see what the steps are to get there. Both approaches can take a structured planned bias or a more emergent one, and they both offer some good outputs that can work. The upside of the incremental approach is that it develops realistic outcomes. The downside is that once you are on the path you have limited options. Because of this I would advocate allowing your analytical mind to wander, to have a little holiday for a moment. Allow your mind to float out into the future 5/10/20/40 years and imagine what your life is like. Where are you living, what do you look like, who is around you in your life, what kind of conversations do you have, what stories do you love to tell? Get specific about the details on the home, the location, the people, and it will give you a compelling goal to work towards. The vision you create tells you some practical things that then enable you to make choices along the way. For instance, if you are sitting on the veranda of a home in the South East of England overlooking the ocean then that comes with a certain price tag. Knowing that means you can work out the kind of income you need to generate for it to become a reality. If you have grandchildren running around the garden then there are some obvious choices that you will have needed to make in terms of having children yourself at some point. Each part of your compelling future vision will give you an indication for today's choices and help when things get tough to drive you onwards towards your goal.

When imagining your future and then getting to the practicalities, there are a few things in life that cannot be changed and need to be considered on your timeline or plan. Acceptance of a few that seem to be universally true can be empowering. One of these is about family, especially for women. I truly feel sad when I am working with a career woman who has been highly successful at work but has now come to a point where she is realising that her choices around whether to have a family are no longer in her hands. Modern science has come a long way and the time window of possibility for you as a woman in fertility terms has been extended, and yet the reality around having a baby is affected by your age. There are many options open to you and age impacts on all of them. As an example of why creating the life you want needs conscious awareness as early as possible, it doesn't get any more real than getting to a point in your life where there is absolutely no possibility of making what you want happen.

STORY

....

Whilst working as the career coach for the Talent Programme in an international charity, I took the approach described above with one of the new incumbents on the programme, Alice. Alice is an intensely driven woman who is a high achiever with even higher standards. Her energy levels are something to behold. She would use every moment of each day for something useful. She'd even listen to university lectures on her Smartphone as she walked to work from the station each day. Her long-term vision in 30 years was clear, and without sharing the full specifics it was looking back over an international career, having collected stories of living in Africa and Asia, and having a family home full of laughter and noise with room for the dogs and the grandchildren to stay. As we drew up Alice's timeline and began to create her compelling vision for 30 years in the future, we chose to chunk the plan down into 10 year and then 5 year periods. This was so that Alice could get really specific and know what she wanted and what was really important to her, and it played to her goal-driven orientation. As we got to the first section from now (32 – 37 years old) I asked Alice when she imagined starting the family that she'd described so graphically in the future. Looking at each of the elements that were required to build the career and life that Alice wanted, we needed to begin prioritising. For the first time it hit her that her 'someday I'll have children' had a shelf-life. If this was truly what she wanted then it needed to become part of the next few years rather than 'someday'. What I love about this story is that Alice then made a conscious choice to go home and have the family conversation, and I'm really happy to say that she and her partner are now the proud parents of a daughter who starts school next year in the International School ... in Nairobi.

EXERCISE

....

Create your own life or career plan

Get a piece of A4 paper and draw the following layout on it –

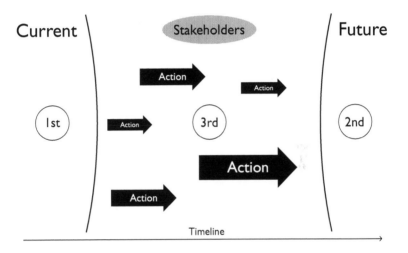

Choose a timeframe that works for you – be sure to make it far enough out to allow your imagination space to create.

Begin by describing your current situation. Consider:

- your environment, where you live, where you work, the atmosphere and cultural vibe

- your skills and capabilities, what you currently do, what you know

- what are the behaviours in your current situation, both yours and those around you at work and at home? How do people act?

- what's currently important to you. What do you believe now?

- who you are. What do you stand for?

Once you have your description of today, rather than jumping straight into action or planning mode we are next going to consider what you want. What's your desired future? What is your compelling vision?

On the right hand side of the page use the same descriptors as for the current situation but begin by describing who you are, what you stand for and then work backwards through the areas until you come to a full picture.

Now is the time to begin to chunk down the timeline into whatever timeframes work for you to be able to ask yourself the questions, "By this stage how will I know I'm on track? What will be true for me now?"

Once you've chunked the timeframe down and considered the questions, then it's time to invite your analytical brain to come back from its holiday and get busy with the action planning.

An additional area to consider when creating your map is, "Who are the key stakeholders?" You may find that they are of great help not only in the delivery of getting started but often in the creation of the vision (especially where it's a life plan you're creating).

Take the time to check in with yourself regularly

Ghandi once said, "There is more to life than increasing its speed", and yet the world today seems to get faster and faster. You have greater access to knowledge and more sources of information at your fingertips than ever before. Time can fly past without your even noticing. If you don't allow space to breathe and reflect, you may wake up one day and wonder how the heck you got to where you are (for good or bad).

> *"If death meant just leaving the stage long enough to change costume and come back as a new character, would you slow down? Or speed up?"*
>
> *Chuck Palahniuk*

If you are constantly in the fast lane, never taking the time to properly refuel or rest, you may find yourself in hot water either physically, emotionally or spiritually. You may have been working really hard climbing your own personal ladder to get on, to improve, to make things happen – only to notice when you get to the top that you had your ladder against the wrong wall.

This danger was shown to me at the first training course I ever went on. I was told the story of the frog in the pan. You may have heard it yourself. It stuck with me and has proved to be true in so many situations that it feels worthy of repeating and sharing… with one word of advice – don't Google the YouTube video story equivalent because it's scary!

If you drop a frog in a pot of boiling water, it will of course frantically try to clamber out. But if you place it gently in a pot of tepid water and turn the heat on low, it will float there quite placidly. As the water gradually heats up, the frog will sink into a tranquil stupor, exactly like someone in a hot bath, and before long, with a smile on its face, it will unresistingly allow itself to be boiled to death.

Version of the story from Daniel Quinn's 'The Story of B'

The human equivalent of the frog may be that over time your hours at work have got longer, or that slowly the pressure valve has been turned up balancing home life and work. Whatever your personal hot water is, the chances are that with some aspects it may have got too hot without you noticing if you don't allow yourself time to step back and take a breath. We become desensitised when things change gradually. So checking in with yourself is a way of mitigating the risk of burning out (or boiling, if you're the frog).

EXERCISE

....

A personal check in

Keep your check-ins light rather than onerous to make the
likelihood of actually doing them higher. Do keep them frequent
enough that, should your metaphorical water be beginning to
get hotter, you notice and choose to hop out before you hit the
stupor stage. Below are a couple of check-in approaches that
I've seen successfully used – if you've got others that work for
you then do share them. I love to hear success stories.

Approach 1 – Diarise and treat your check-in reflection time
like any other maintenance appointment. You probably go for
a dental check up every 6-12 months or for a haircut every 6
weeks, so book the time in your diary every 3 to 6 months to
simply stop, take a breath, notice what's in your life and which
direction you're heading and ask yourself is it working for you.

Approach 2 – Take a piece of paper and draw the following
grid:

	Importance 1-10	Energy 1-10	Satisfaction 1-10
Social – e.g. family, friends, holidays			
Emotional – e.g. doing the things you enjoy, connecting			
Intellectual – e.g. reading, writing, learning, training			
Spiritual – e.g. meditate, visit a gallery, volunteer			
Physical – e.g. exercise, diet, rest and relaxation, sleep			

Ask yourself for each category the three questions:

- How important to me is this area of my life?

- How much energy do I currently put into this area?

- Right now how satisfied am I with this area of my life?

Mark your level of importance, energy and satisfaction on a scale of 1 to 10, with 1 being not at all and 10 being the most you can imagine. Notice the balance between the scores you've given. Are you placing your energy where you have said things are most important? Where are your pinch points and what could you do to change things? Or are you satisfied with how things are in that area at the moment? If so, then know that you can relax into continuing to do what you are currently doing and place your energy elsewhere.

....

You have what it takes to create the life you want

Within each of us we hold the answers. You may need help, encouragement, challenge and to learn from others along the way... but it's important to know that you are the person that is best placed to know what will work best for you. Trusting yourself and having the resilience to continue are key to creating satisfaction in your life.

Say no to deflators and distractors

For many of you it may be an inner drive to please that means that you have a seemingly auto response of 'Yes, of course' to any request. This may then be followed with a moment of 'OMG how will I deliver on that?' or an acknowledgement that you will now be putting in another 12 hour day. When the phone rings or someone turns up at your desk, that is the moment to break the pattern, to STOP for just a second and consider your options BEFORE you respond! It's likely that you may have been having the knee-jerk response of 'yes' for a long time, so simply knowing that you need to change it is unlikely to be enough to break the pattern.

STORY

The most effective way of making the change was demonstrated to me not by a single client but by a whole smattering of team members from a global telecoms company I was working with. I had been running a series of 'Espresso' sessions for them and found myself feeling much like a member of the team as I was at their offices pretty regularly. Now don't get confused by the name. 'Espresso' sessions weren't about coffee drinking. They were a short, funky and powerful approach to workshops. We'd get together for just three hours and with lots of energy and experiences learn some stuff on topics from Making Meetings Matter to Living with Change. One workshop was about Staying on Top of Things, and the 12 people that joined me for the session were keen to learn how to say no (without being rude). Without breaching the confidentiality of the details of individuals' reasons for having an automated yes response, I can share a common theme that emerged – habit; a habit that had begun because they wanted to do a good job and for them that meant taking on whatever was thrown at them and delivering – whatever the cost. At the workshop I shared a STOP tool (see below) by Tim Gallwey with whom I've had the privilege of training in London. (He's an inspiring man in his 70s who can still outrun me on a tennis court and is one of the best coaches I've come across.) On a trip back to the offices I bumped into someone from the workshop. He took me by the hand and led me to the marketing floor where what I saw brought a huge smile to my face. Around the open plan desks many now had a picture of a STOP road sign next to the phone. Tim who was showing me this shared with me that since the workshop the team had managed to create an atmosphere of support that included considering timelines and impacts before saying yes to requests... and it hadn't impacted on how they were viewed in terms of their service to internal customers at all. He was particularly happy because he was now getting to leave the office on time more regularly and got home to read a bedtime story to his little boy.

Saying no can bring gravitas and help you reclaim time to prioritise what's really important to you. Listening to supporters and avoiding the deflators focusses your attention on what you want and what will make a real difference – to you, to your team and to your organisation.

EXERCISE

The STOP tool

Imagine for a moment that you are a Roman general charging on your horse into battle with your troops behind you. You come up against a wall, a high wall that you cannot see over. What do you do?

Jump it?

Go around it?

Knock it over?

There are many answers to the question but many could lead to loss of life. If you don't slow down to see what's over the wall before you leap, there could be enemy troops lying in wait!

Instead, STOP. Step back so you can see over the wall and, at the same time, see your own soldiers as well as the massed ranks of the enemy on the other side of the wall.

Your daily life is unlikely to be a battlefield and yet at times it may feel as pressured. Stopping helps you to take your finger off the fast forward button of life as you rush through it. Stopping you from ploughing on regardless, from being driven ever faster by life's demands and the pressures of modern technology. Pausing in a world where you are always available, anywhere – because of mobile phones. Tuning out for a moment from the fire hose of information and spam coming from road markings, the TV, the phone, the internet, the post, the reports... and the list goes on... ... ...

Step back
So you can see over the wall

Think
Notice your options, and set goals

Organise
Plan and communicate the next steps

Proceed
Do what you've decided and planned to do

Ref Tim Gallwey

"To take time to think is to gain time to live" –

Nancy Kline

What you admire in others, you have within you

To see something in another person, you have to first know what it is. To know what it is, you must have experienced it before. To have experienced it before, then the first time had to be within yourself, even if it was for just a moment. If you have no knowledge of something, then you cannot have the words or emotions to be able to describe it. We even have things called mirror neurons in our brain that many cognitive psychologists would say are the key to how we learn through imitation (amongst many other things). A mirror neuron is one that reacts, fires off if you will, when an animal does something and then observes the same action being performed by another animal. Many tests have been conducted with primates to begin to understand this phenomenon and to explore how this may be useful for treating things like autism. For most of you though, it's an interesting piece of information that, without having to understand the science in detail, you might want to consider in terms of who you are, how you act and the perceptions and impacts you create in others. Becoming the best version of yourself begins with believing that you have it all within you already. Being able to make choices starts with knowing what's important to you, what's of value.

Know where you want to be and who
you want to be on the way

EXERCISE

....

Heroes and Villains

Step 1 – Make a list of the top five people you admire and the top five people you dislike. They can be real or fictional, past or present, known well or at a distance. Draw representations of them on a large sheet of paper (flipchart if you have one).

Step 2 – Identify the characteristics, capabilities or attributes of each person that you admire them for or dislike them for. Illustrate your pictures with symbols or images which capture these and the strength of your feelings.

Step 3 – For each person you admire, ask: which values do they represent? For each person you dislike ask: which values does he/she violate?

Step 4 – Ask: what does this tell me about the values that are important to me?

....

Self-affirmation works

If you believe what others say about you, why don't you think about what you say about you to yourself? Maybe you have already considered it and maybe you are your own best cheerleader. If that's true then brilliant. For a number of you though, you may have an inner voice that is less than supportive at times, one that might call you stupid or not good enough. I've worked with some senior managers in FTSE 100 companies who have an inner voice telling them that they'll get caught out one day. A Director of Communications I was working with had a voice telling him that he wasn't director material and asking who was he to say no when others asked for his time. This meant that he was loved by his team because he was seen to be always available, but it meant that his diary had no space to do any work, to allow him space to think, even to give him time to sort through the bag of paperwork he'd been carrying to and from work every day for over a week. The consequences were widespread as he wasn't getting to see his young family as much as he wanted so he felt like a bad father, and at the same time he was being perceived at work as a doer not a strategic thinker so he was not hitting his goals there either.

The inner voice has power and it's your voice (most of the time). Because it's your voice and it's in your head this means you can teach it to say good things that are motivational or allow it to continue to criticise.

What you say to yourself leaks out in your physiology, how you hold your body. Your physical presence gets judged by others. As a human being you make meaning of what you see based on all sorts of assumptions. A common one might be that when you see someone with slightly rounded shoulders, holding themselves back and keeping their head low, they are shy or weak in some way. It might be in their tone of voice or their handshake even – think David Beckham in the 90s before his voice coaching lowered his tone an octave, or remember that wet fish handshake from that meeting you went to. Both set the tone for what you think of a person and both will be connected to what you say to yourself about them and you.

STORY

This connection became really apparent to me when working with a career coaching client, Kim. She was preparing for an interview within her organisation but outside her area of experience. She had been working in risk management and auditing and had made a decision that she wanted to follow the passion that she had for working with young people. Before we got into the complexities of interview preparation and CV analysis I was keen to understand what Kim's inner voice was saying to her about the shift. So I asked her, "Why do you want to do youth work?" Her response, even without hearing the words, was so apologetic that it told me that at that moment she didn't believe that she could get the job...that she was more than likely saying to herself unhelpful things such as 'I've got no qualifications in this field' or 'why would they employ someone with so little experience'. Now, these may be useful things to prepare answers around but they are not useful things to be saying over and over to yourself internally.

Through repetition Kim created an affirmation that spoke of her passion for creating healthy communities and her beliefs that our youth are at the heart of that. What was remarkable, while watching her as she practiced making her new statement out loud, was that every time she said it she literally stood taller. She became bigger, and therefore looked more confident, right before my eyes. As a recruiting manager I know which version of Kim I'd be more likely to hire.

What's useful to know about the connection between what we say to ourselves, our bodies and others' judgments is that, by changing either our physiology or what we say, we can have an immediate impact. So stand up straight, take a deep breath and create your own positive affirmation using the tool below... and repeat as required until you believe it!

EXERCISE

....

Self-Affirmations – Story Editing

As it's your story you can say anything in it you choose. One way of editing your story that has been shown to effectively change how people handle illness through to handling personal happiness is:

1. Think about an area of your life that you value, e.g. religion, athletics, family, musical ability, relationships...

2. Pick the area that is most important to you from your list.

3. Write about a time when that area of your life was particularly important and why.

Simple as that! A really brief writing exercise that only takes a few minutes, and focusses your brain onto what's truly important to you and for you.

You may want to begin to practice self-affirmation daily. If that's something you would enjoy, then from your story consider a short statement that you could say to yourself each morning to focus on what's important. Some that I've heard and know work are:

• I feel happy, healthy and great.

• I believe in myself and my ability to do anything I set my mind to.

- I let go of any need to seek others' approval.

- We do the best we can with the resources we have.

- I am a driven and courageous person.

Create your own affirmation including roles that are important to you like mum, leader or coach.

....

The map is not the territory

One of my favourite subjects at school was geography. I loved nothing more than spending time pouring over maps. Checking out the contour lines and the names of places. Imagining what each village and town might be like. Noticing how green or built up areas were and considering how many pubs and churches seem to populate rural areas. So when I mention the map not being the territory you may think that I am being literal. In some ways I am, but mostly I'm thinking metaphorically. Even when I remember letting my imagination run wild, because it was the days before Google maps' Street View, I didn't know what the village high street looked like, or whether the top of the hills marked as green spaces were heavily wooded or moorland. Real maps don't tell us everything about a territory. They may be useful guides but they are not the whole truth. In the same way the maps that you create for yourself throughout your life, about life itself and being human, where you live, who you are, the kind of relationships that work or don't, what is appropriate behaviour in situations ... and the list goes on... These maps don't tell us the whole story either and they are certainly not the truth.

Your map is different from everyone else's

Our lives are so different and yet we may fail to notice or think more widely than our own small plot of land.

Growing up in West Cornwall in a small town where everyone knew each other's names was a very different experience from the street kids I met whilst visiting Umthombo, a street kids' charity in Durban, on a fundraising visit a few years ago. Their maps and reality were of violence, poverty and survival where women and girls were to be traded not cherished. My map growing up, although traditional in many ways, was one of equality and safety. But you don't have to have been born in different countries to have different maps, you might even come from the same town or the same family and have different experiences of life in the same environment. Sitting in the place you are right now as you read this book, you will be having a different experience to the person sitting next to you. If you are alone, move to the other side of the room and your perspective will change. At any one given moment there are over 2,000,000,000 bps (bits per second) of information occurring around us. Your brain has a phenomenal filtering system that enables you to operate in a world with so much going on because brains can only handle up to 134 bps. That's a whopping 1,999,999,866 bits of information that we filter out. So the likelihood of everyone at the same time having the same experience filtering for the same 134 bits is highly unlikely. This being our inbuilt way of being in the world means that each and every one of us has to build our own unique maps of our world because we see, hear and feel a different 134 bits per second.

Your reference points or experiences are the things that, when you build your map, guide you. They are what enable you to make decisions, to make choices. Those choices either consciously or unconsciously are driven by your values (what's important to us) and your beliefs (those things that we 'know' to be true). Your beliefs hang off your values and they drive your behaviours and so set you off on particular paths each and every day. Like sheep in the countryside, if you go down the same pathways often enough you create a 'sheep trail' – a pathway that you get stuck in – a groove that becomes habitual. Sometimes this can be really useful as it means you do things without thought. However, as you learn and grow through life, often the grooves or sheep trails that worked 10 years ago may not be taking you in the right direction today.

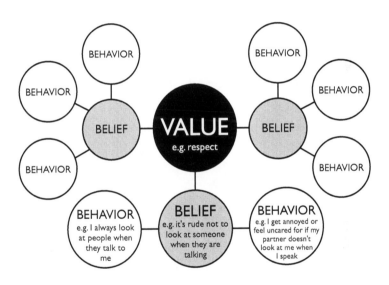

A value that I hold dear is concerned with respect. Treating others as I would like to be treated is the way my parents used to express it to me as a child. You may have grown up in a similar household or you may hold respect up as something that's important for you too. If you do, then it can be interesting to consider what are the beliefs that come from your values concerning respect and what behaviours they drive as well as if they are working for you?

STORY

A few years ago I was attending an evening seminar with my husband that a friend was running about the psychology of sales. We were there mostly in support of Alison as it was her first time running a seminar solo and also because the subject matter was interesting to both of us, being self-employed and having to sell our wares to earn a living. We were around 20 minutes into the seminar when I could feel myself quietly brewing and getting irritated by my husband Marcus because he was on his iPhone when, in my view, he should have been watching and listening to Alison – it was disrespectful of Marcus being on his phone whilst she was speaking. Because his actions were crossing one of my values, my internal reaction was strong as you can imagine. I was thinking all sorts of 'how can he'-type things and doing a really good job of winding myself up. Then about 30 minutes into the seminar Alison asked a question of the audience. It was time for us to participate. To be able to participate you really had to have been learning from what she'd been sharing from the stage, so I was thinking 'there's no way Marcus can now get involved – he's letting us down'… and then he asked the most amazing question of Alison that he wouldn't have been able to ask if he hadn't been fully engaged for the previous full 30 minutes. Now this made me curious. How did he do that and why was I having such a strong reaction? After much pondering I realised that linked to my 'respect' value I had a 'look-to-listen' rule running as a belief about how you demonstrate your respect for others. By a look-to-listen rule I mean that I believed that for you to be listening to me you must be looking at me. If you are currently nodding your head or thinking, yup, that's right, people are only listening when they look at you, then the chances are that you, like me, grew up in a household where one or other parent said to you, "Look at me when I'm talking to you". Hearing that often enough from someone close to you when you are a child builds the belief, and we believe it to be fact. Not everyone grows up with a parent who says that to them. My husband definitely didn't. His youth was much more flexible and creatively biased. He often describes it as free range, and so he has no such look-to-listen rule running. In fact, for him to be able to listen and take things in fully he needs to be looking away, either out of the window or at his phone, so that he isn't distracted by the visual impact of the speaker. His brain is wired in a non-linear way that means when having multiple areas at work simultaneously he is concentrating more. So, these are two very different ways of viewing the world that impact on day-to-day life and the meaning we make of it.

TIP:

The next time you get irritated by or notice your beliefs are different from someone else's, instead of reacting or persuading, pop on your curiosity spectacles and ask: "What would need to be true for me to believe that or to act in that way?"

Perception is reality

What you see, hear and feel is all you really have to go on in this
world in terms of making sense of what's happening around
you. Your perceptions become your reality because they are
your experience. At the same time they are not reality in and
of itself because of the filtering systems you read about earlier
in this chapter. Remember the 2,000,000,000 bits per second of
which you only take in 134? Add to this filtering the notion
that as a human being you are hardwired to not want to be
wrong, so you filter the world looking for examples that make
your perceptions right.

STORY

In 2007 I was doing a race for charity across Africa in a 1969
VW Beetle with my great friend Rachel. On one particular
day, filtering had a huge impact on me emotionally. We
had by this time already driven coast to coast across South
Africa, had driven through Namibia and were venturing
into Botswana. The roads were more rocky dirt tracks as
we were heading into some pretty remote areas. As I drove
through what might be described as a village, I noticed
small children, only half clothed, begging by the side of the
road. We had been warned that in some areas these children
were being used to draw in travellers, and then the adults
would arrive and take anything of value from you so we
knew not to stop. This didn't make it any less upsetting
to see, and because it affected me all I could then see as we
continued were more and more examples of abject poverty
and hungry children. Luckily my friend Rachel is a really

talented coach and she began asking me questions to broaden my vision from the begging children. As my filters fell from my eyes I became able to notice the other children that we were driving past. Their pristine school uniforms, almost glowing white shirts, and the smiles on their faces as they walked home after a day of study, all living in the mud huts in the village but happy and healthy.

Your perceptions, like mine in Africa, can be skewed in the moment by something you see and connect with, or they may be habitually set because of life experiences so far. It's good to know that perceptions aren't necessarily reality and to begin to ask yourself, "What else might be true here, what am I missing?"

TIP:

Stay true to who you are and be open to possibility. Authentic and flexible wins over fake and solid both over time and every time.

Weather changes both the map and the territory

If you have ever spent time on moorland you will know this statement to be true. In my 20s I lived on Dartmoor and one of the draws and downsides of being there was the ever-changing landscape. One moment the sun could be shining and you could see as far as the coast and in a heartbeat the fog could set in and you could no longer see right in front of you.

Storms and sunshine happen both in weather systems and life. Some days it may be that you need to have remembered to take your umbrella with you and on others it's just to get inside fast or choose to get wet. Whatever the occurrence, the key is to be prepared and have your eyes open to what's happening in order to be able to choose your action. Sometimes in life stresses and pressures build up over time and other times they are a little more like a tsunami or tornado that seems to appear from nowhere. When changes happen, the first step is often to accept the change, not roll over and give up but acknowledge that things are now different.

As a unique individual you will have different sources of stress to others. For some of you having a full email inbox and a long job list may be stressful, and for others it can be motivating to power on through it. What can be empowering and useful is to understand what may cause stress for you, and to learn what you could do to minimize that stress. One challenge when wanting to manage pressure is the really thin line between when something is a stretching challenge and when it tips you over the edge into strain and overwhelms you. The better able you are to notice your own early warning indicators, the earlier you can do something to avoid stress.

'Stress: the adverse reaction people have to excessive pressures or other types of demands placed upon them'.

Health and Safety Executive

Although the HSE definition of stress works when you are thinking of stress as the overwhelmed, out-of-control and strained version when things get too much, it doesn't take into account positive stress. Yes, positive stress – the kind of stress that is required to make a bridge strong, the awareness of the pressure points to be able to place the keystone to hold the bridge up safely for years to come. You have your own pressure points that will be motivational and make you stronger. The key may be to know where your own boundary is between the positive stress and falling over, and to build up your muscles in times of less stress so that you are strong enough when the pressure comes.

EXERCISE
....

Stress Indicators

Let's find out what your early indicators are for stress. The list below is not exhaustive so do use it as a stimulus for you to consider your personal stress indicators.

Tick off those that might apply for you and add others that arise.

PHYSICAL
- ❑ Loss of appetite or overeating
- ❑ Headaches
- ❑ Muscle aches
- ❑ Tension
- ❑ Disturbed sleep/insomnia
- ❑ Tiredness/fatigue
- ❑ Weight loss or gain
- ❑ Susceptibility to colds
- ❑ Stomach pains, sickness, diarrhoea
- ❑ Pounding heart
- ❑ Accident prone
- ❑ Teeth grinding
- ❑ Restlessness and irritability
- ❑ Foot-tapping/finger-drumming
- ❑ Increasing alcohol, drug or tobacco use
- ❑ Worsening of underlying medical conditions eg. Rashes, skin problems

MENTAL/INTELLECTUAL
- ❑ Poor memory
- ❑ Poor sensory awareness
- ❑ Poor concentration and focus
- ❑ Low productivity

❑ No new ideas

❑ Negative or 'don't care' attitude

❑ Disorganised, confused and unprepared

SPIRITUAL

❑ Loss of meaning, direction and purpose

❑ Doubt

❑ Unforgiving

❑ Martyrdom

❑ Looking for magic

❑ Needing to 'prove' yourself

❑ Cynicism

❑ Apathy and unwillingness to commit

EMOTIONAL

❑ Anxiety

❑ Worry

❑ Frustration

❑ Irritability

❑ Mood swings

❑ Bad temper/angry outbursts

❑ Crying spells, and feeling weepy

❑ Feeling isolated

❑ Depression or the 'blues'

❑ Nervous breakdowns

SOCIAL

❑ Seeks isolation and being alone/hidden

❑ Intolerance

❑ Increasing arguments at home and work

❑ Lashing out

❑ Avoids communicating

❑ Lowered sex drive

❑ Lack of intimacy

❑ Nagging

❑ Distrust

- ❑ Fewer contacts with friends
- ❑ withdrawn
- ❑ Lethargy
- ❑ Boredom
- ❑ Spacing-out or 'losing the plot'
- ❑ Negative self-talk

Next, notice if there is any bias towards any particular category? Are your responses primarily physical, or are you someone who socially withdraws and reacts?

Knowing your indicators and being able to describe them can help you and others around you to manage your pressure early and in a positive way.

....

What we believe to be true changes

At one point in your life you most likely believed in the tooth fairy, and if we go back to the early 13th century you most likely would have believed that the world was flat. Things change either because of new discoveries and learning, or because you mature and grow. Being a 40 year-old who still believes in the tooth fairy is probably not the way to a satisfying and successful life, but being 6 and believing can be quite magical. Different beliefs are for different times in life, and being flexible enough to remember that things change is healthy.

Belief and truth are different

Set yourself free from pressure and inner conflict right now by allowing yourself to know this to be possible. If you hold beliefs and truths to be one and the same, you may have the satisfaction of feeling right, but the likelihood is that there are many people who would love to prove you wrong, or you limit the circle of people in your life because they must believe what you do to fit in. Either way is of course your choice and neither is right or wrong in and of itself. What you may want to consider is adding the word 'yet' to some of your thoughts and beliefs. "I'm not fit enough to run a marathon – yet", or, "I don't have enough experience in managing people to apply for that promotion – yet". Say to yourself both versions with and without the 'yet' and notice how different they feel. One is static and a statement of fact (seemingly) and the other has a sense of reality and possibility at the same time. I know which I would prefer to live with and which I've seen make the difference to the lives of people that I work with.

truth

1. the <u>true</u> or actual state of a matter: *He tried to find out the truth.*

2. conformity with fact or reality; verity: *the truth of a statement.*

3. a verified or indisputable fact, proposition, principle, or the like: *mathematical truths.*

4. the state or character of being <u>true.</u>

5. actuality or actual existence.

belief

1. something <u>believed</u>; an opinion or conviction: *a belief that the earth is flat.*

2. confidence in the truth or existence of something not immediately susceptible to rigorous proof: *a statement unworthy of belief.*

3. confidence; faith; trust: *a child's belief in his parents.*

4. a religious tenet or tenets; religious <u>creed</u> or faith: *the Christian belief.*

Opposing views can be true at the same time

In the 21ˢᵗ century we live in a world of dualism. One where opposites are used to help us make sense of the world, for example, Black/White, Good/Bad, Pain/Pleasure, Emergent/Planned, Mechanistic/Organic... the list is endless. It can be hugely challenging to consider that someone or something can be both good and bad at the same time or that pleasure and pain can also be simultaneous. Once you begin to allow yourself to let go of control and certainty, your world will open up before you.

Conflict is often a result of a tightly held dualism, a belief that if one thing is true the other cannot be. What one person sees as spontaneous, another may see as reckless or lazy because, in their map of the world, things are either planned or chaotic. I've seen many an argument stem from this type of thinking both in a work and home context.

EXERCISE

. . . .

Conflict Resolution – seeing the world through someone else's eyes

First set up three chairs facing each other. One is for you, one for the person/people you have the conflict with, and the third is for the you that can objectively view the conflict from outside the situation.

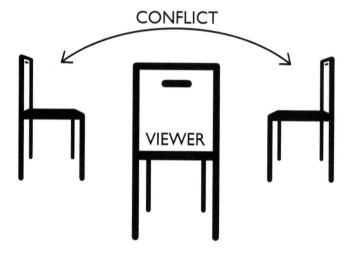

1. Sit in the first chair and express your opinion, feelings and thoughts as if you are speaking to the other person.

2. Break your state – stand up and shake it off, walk around the room, have a laugh at something if you like.

3. Sit in the other chair and express the other person's opinion as if they are talking to you. You may not know exactly what they are thinking or feeling, but go with what comes to you and what you believe might be going on for them. It can sometimes help to sit the way they might sit in the chair as it uses the memory and imagination in a different way.

4. Repeat having heard what each side had to say.

Having had this experience first, notice what you observe in terms of how it feels for you now.

Next, sit in the middle chair and determine:

- What are the positive intentions of both sides? What is their need in the situation for the good?

- What beliefs might be running that are keeping the conflict alive?

- What physical feelings are present in each individual? Notice where in the body this is and tense and relax the areas of tension.

- As you look to each party (the other chairs), talk out and imagine what is now possible in the conversation.

Holding on too tight can kill

Although war and violence are complex at an individual psychological level, there are commonalities that strike me whenever some horror hits the news. The drivers behind most of the conflicts, particularly where religious beliefs are stated as the reason, stem from tightly held beliefs and interpretations. What I notice about the individuals committing the atrocities, whether it's the 7/7 bombings in London or the many terrorist attacks over the years, is that those involved are fundamentalists first and then Muslim/Christian/Jewish/Protestant or whatever it may be, second. They have more in common with each other than those who wear the same religious 'badge'.

Photo taken of work by street artist Ben Slow in East London

STORY

At the time of the 7/7 bombings in London I was working in a corporate role on the top floor of an office block on the Marylebone Road very close to the site of where one of the bombs went off. I remember the confusion and panic that ensued so clearly it could have been yesterday. In the following days and weeks, when the beliefs of the bombers came to light and why it was they had felt they had to commit such a crime against humanity, a thought struck me about the fundamentalist nature of the attack. The bomb that went off at Edgware Road was set by one of the four Islamic home-grown terrorists claiming it was in the name of Islam – and Edgware Road is one of the most heavily populated areas for Muslim/Islamic people in London: an example for me that the bombing could not have been about religious beliefs but fundamentalist behaviour in the most extreme way.

The ripple effect was felt for months afterwards by a friend of mine who is of Pakistani descent and British by birth. She worked in the City in a management role, so dressed smartly, and had used the tube to commute for years. Following the attacks she found that whenever she boarded a train people moved away from her. Questioning looks and nervous glances had a big impact on her and caused her to begin to suffer from panic attacks and a sense of being completely out of control of her life. The assumptions and generalisations of others at an instinctive survival level caused further damage way beyond 7/7!

These are extreme examples of holding on too tightly to beliefs and the impact it can have. Every day you will hold opinions and make assumptions at an unconscious level. You may be aware of their impact on yourself and others, or you may not. Becoming aware will enable you to choose to let go. Spend time reflecting or begin to pay attention to how you go about your day. What are you making your decisions on and how tightly are you holding onto what you believe to be true?

Flexibility is key

One constant in 21st century living is that things are changing continually. Whether it's the shape of our organisations, the skyline of our major cities or what's deemed to be healthy in terms of lifestyle, it's all change. Living well today may be more about how flexible we are to be able to adapt than ever before. Living with change, rather than managing change, seems much more useful as a thing to learn. A subtle but powerful difference in nuance.

> *"It is not the strongest of the species that survives, nor the most intelligent, but the one most responsive to change."*
>
> *Charles Darwin*

In nature we find examples of strength in flexibility everywhere. In high winds the willow wins over the mighty oak, and in the rushing of the stream the water separates to flow around the rocks rather than being stopped by the obstacles. Going with the flow can empower and strengthen you in times of change. For those of you who enjoy the sense of structure and control that comes with a good plan, the notion of fluidity may be a challenge... and may be one to build into your toolkit to build your resilience. Remember it's not a dualism, it's not fluid or solid, it can be both. Mother Nature creates healthy trees in which the root system spreads far out in all directions, giving the tree stability and enabling it to draw its nutrients from over a wide area. If one of these roots is temporarily weakened, broken or dries up, the others will be strong enough to keep the tree alive and upright. I saw this in action when the Victorian water mains were being replaced on our street and I could see when I looked into the hole that a London Plane tree's roots had been cut through, and yet the tree remained healthy as those roots under the pavement were not touched.

In your own life imagine the tree's root system from the story represents the key areas in your life. To be truly healthy, like the tree, you must draw nutrients from all areas. Periodically, thinking consciously about the key areas of your life enables you to target your energies to those parts that you may be at risk of losing, or enable you to choose to cut them off.

The goal is for you to notice and make a choice before any area hits rock bottom. The choice is up to you, and it's the timing of any change that can make all the difference.

EXERCISE

....

Life Balance Wheel

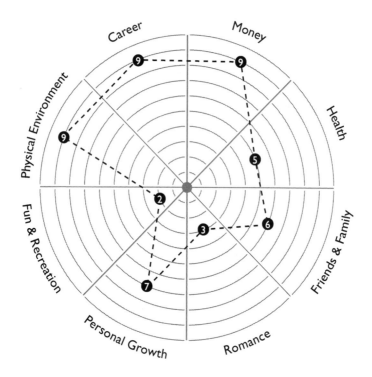

Lives are complex, and it can be easy for time to fly past and for the many different roles and areas of importance to get out of balance. This exercise is designed to give you the opportunity to take a snapshot of where you are today to enable you to consciously make choices for tomorrow.

1. Put each of the key areas of your life on a separate spoke of the wheel. Examples have been provided; however, you can change them if they don't work for you.

2. Rate your satisfaction with each, using a scale of 1 (low) to 10 (high) by placing a mark on the scale. Remember, it's satisfaction not achievement we're looking at. You could have achieved a huge amount and not be satisfied and equally you could be achieving little but be really satisfied.

3. Connect the marks on each scale by drawing lines between them to give you a 'plan' of your state of balance right now.

4. Take a look at your balance wheel. Will it give you a smooth or a bumpy ride through life? It's not just the shape that you need to notice, it's the size too. Small wheels tend to get caught in ruts in the road!

5. Consider the next steps for you. Which areas are sufficiently important to you that you are willing to invest energy in making changes? What might the changes be that close the gap between how you actually spend your time and what really matters to you?

There is no such thing as a perfect balance in life – life is just too fluid and dynamic for that. Knowing your current shape of wheel enables you to make choices and decide if you want to set some goals in deficient areas. If you do decide to take some actions to redress your balance, then repeat the exercise in 3 months' time to see how you're doing. You might even want to complete the exercise with a partner so you can come up with joint goals.

CHAPTER 4

Anything is possible…

On any journey you need a start point and a destination. Whether it's ordering a taxi to take you to a restaurant, or the more philosophical journeys in life, you need to be able to describe where you are today and the direction you want to go. You may hit roadblocks or diversions or simply run out of fuel on the way. The knack is in knowing that, whatever happens, anything is possible… and that may need to include accepting your start point. For some of you it may be that your start point, like mine, is a council estate where ambition isn't exactly a celebrated thing, or it may be that, like one of my great friends Rebecca, you are from a privileged background but want to be known for your own successes, not the reflected glory from your family… or somewhere in between. Whatever your start point, one thing is certain, it is what it is! So you have a choice – you can accept it, call your taxi and head off, or you can pretend your start point is somewhere else, live in denial and frustration, and the taxi won't be able to find you to get you started on your way to a new destination. The choice of approach is yours.

Your inner critic may want to disagree

"Anything is possible…"

As a statement you may find that the voice in your head, the inner critic, kicks in saying something like, "No it's not!" or, "Here we go, tree-huggy optimist stuff". Now you may even be saying to yourself right now, "What does she mean, inner critic? I don't have one of those, I've no inner voices in my head!" Well, if that's you then the voice I'm talking about is the very one that is saying you don't have one – that's the voice I'm talking about.

Make friends with your inner critic – it gets results

Thinking of our inner critic as a person can be a helpful way to consider how to handle it. If you had someone standing in front of you telling you that you couldn't do something, or that you were daft, I'm sure you'd listen and react accordingly. Your reaction may depend on the intention behind the words and actions of the person, but you would react and they would respond. For example, if you choose to argue they may well fight back, if you choose to ask questions to understand their perspective then they're likely to engage with you, or if you choose to ignore them then they are likely to get louder until you listen.

Your inner voice can be handled effectively by taking a similar approach, and that means the first thing you need to do is to understand the intention behind what it's saying.

As a human being, survival is hardwired into you, and so it could be safe to assume that anything you do or think comes from a baseline of wanting something good for yourself. It's likely to be positively intended. That doesn't mean that the action or way that you speak to yourself manifests in a useful, kind or positive way, or even that the approach will work. You might actually sound like you're being rude if your voice says things like, "Don't even try, you're too stupid to get it right", or, "They won't like you, you're too fat/old/short...". Knowing that the voice has a good intention behind the words means that a good place to start with your inner voice is to seek to understand what it is trying to achieve by being quite so critical about you. The alternative options to ignore it, tell it to shut up or have an argument with it, all take huge amounts of energy and don't usually take you forward. If you ignore it you may find it gets louder, if you tell it to shut up you most likely will end up with an internal row, and if you go headlong into arguing with yourself then there can be no ultimate winner, just a waste of energy.

STORY

....

I was working with a brand manager, Tom, at a world-renowned beverage company and his inner critic had been busy. We were having a conversation about long-term career goals and aspirations, and Tom seemed really stuck in his thinking. This was pretty unusual for him as typically he's creative and driven and is someone who is seen as a future leader of the organisation – he has what it takes to get on. As we talked, I noticed that whenever I asked him to think further than two years ahead he seemed to go into himself, which made me curious. So I asked him to stop and notice what he was saying to himself. As I suspected, his inner critic was telling him that there was no point long-term planning because his career was in the hands of his bosses anyway. He was then embarking on an internal intellectual battle between the part of him that believed he was responsible for his own success and the other part that didn't. In that moment I asked him to take a second, just a breath, and to step back from the internal dialogue and ask a different question of himself. "What is my inner critic's intention in telling me that my bosses hold all the power? What is its intended outcome?" After a few moments considering this, Tom shared with me that the intention of his inner critic was to protect him from failure. If he believed his bosses had the power then he couldn't fail. Being protected is a good thing but at the same time it was having a negative impact. It was stopping Tom from being able to see clearly where he wanted his career to go, let alone apply for jobs to get him there. So, by finding other ways to mitigate the fear of failure, we were able to move on and take action. Something that we wouldn't have been able to do if we hadn't befriended the critic to understand what it was trying to achieve.

EXERCISE

....

Conversations with your inner critic

Week 1 – Over the coming week open your ears to your inner voice. Without judgment, allow it to say what it wants to say and simply write it down.

Week 2 – After a week of capturing what your inner voice is saying, allow yourself to get curious. Ask your inner voice (as if it's another person) what is the intention behind what it is saying. Then simply thank it.

Week 3 – Notice any changes that may have occurred in how your inner voice talks to you and/or what it's saying. If some of the statements remain, then it's time to ask the creative part of you for some ideas as to how else you might achieve the intention of the inner voice but in a more effective way.

Week 4 – Notice now what your inner voice is saying. Offer thanks and reassurance if you want to. Create new things for your inner voice to say that you would find empowering or uplifting in some way.

....

A loud inner voice can be motivating – the critic versus the cheerleader

Your motivations will be different from others' and yet there will be those who have similar buttons that get them going. With fitness, for instance, I'm motivated by the end results and by having some fun along the way, whereas my friend Alison is hugely motivated by the 'bootcamp' approach to fitness and goes the extra mile when someone is screaming at her, sergeant major-style. If she used my strategy of imagining the end result, she'd never get started, and if I took her approach, I'd end up crying or screaming back. Knowing whether you are someone who is naturally drawn 'towards' goals or someone who prefers to move 'away' from what they don't want is important when it comes to managing yourself and others. It's a pattern of thinking that will unconsciously affect the decisions and choices you make.

STORY

A classic example of how a 'towards' bias when overused can be a hindrance came up when working with Alana, an HR professional from the construction industry who worked across contracts that went from the military to commerce. Her challenge was with Bob, the MD of one of the group of companies that primarily dealt with military contracts. There was an issue in Bob's business where two of the key senior managers weren't operating in an aligned way, and the effect was that by achieving their own goals they were impacting on each other's areas in a detrimental way. Bob was struggling to have any influence in this area and Alana came to me to explore how she might best support him in leading and managing his people more effectively. As we looked at the details of what approaches had been taken so far, it became apparent to me that both Bob and Alana had a clear 'towards' bias in terms of motivation. To get either of them engaged or motivated to take action, a carrot approach was needed. To describe the rewards and the positive outcomes once things had changed would drive them to get started, and so they had been deploying this style as their motivational approach with the senior managers. They had made it clear that change was needed, but had been using outcome and solution-based language to attempt to engage the senior managers...to very little effect! Both the managers in question appeared to have a tendency to describe the worst-case scenarios and were incredibly good risk managers as a result (a very useful trait given the nature of the military contracts they worked on). This gave us an indication that Bob and Alana needed to switch to talking about the problems that would be faced as a result of being unaligned as a management team, describing the negative impacts on both them and the organisation as a whole if they continued operating in the same way. The key was to give both the managers something to move 'away from', to give them their own worst-case scenario picture.

You might have different preferred motivational strategies at play in different areas of your life. It may be that imagining the sunny days out on the golf course, or playing with the grandchildren, motivates you to pay into your pension and keep working hard, whereas you may find that when it comes to health and fitness you experience the opposite. You may be more like Alison, with her boot camp approach and the image of a fat, slobby, couch potato version of herself in her mind's eye. Both different and both effective – as long as they play to your preference in that area. Or it may be that the idea of poverty in old age is your motivator for having a pension, but feeling healthy and looking great in your jeans is your fitness strategy.

Noticing what your drivers and those of others are can make you a truly adaptable and effective leader. Whether you're leading an organisation, a family or yourself, being able to hit the 'towards' or 'away from' motivational button at the right time will take you closer to your goals.

EXERCISE

Your motivational style

Knowing whether you are drawn towards something and want more of it in your life, or whether you are driven to stop something happening, has an impact on how you behave in that area of your life on a daily basis.

1. Ask yourself the following question for each area of your life, e.g. career:

   "In the context of ..., can you remember a time when you were totally motivated? Can you remember a specific time?"

2. Take yourself back to that time and re-experience it. As you remember this time, what was the last thing you felt, just before you were totally motivated? Give that feeling a name, e.g. excitement.

3. What's important about that (e.g. excitement) to you?

As you answer the questions, notice whether your answers are about becoming closer to or having more of something, or are about avoiding something.

Once you know your motivations, you can begin to use them proactively either to get yourself to do something or to sort through your options more quickly. For instance, if your top five were *results, satisfaction, fun, fulfilment* and *money*, then you may want to set your goals using these as triggers. To sell something to yourself, you would need to hear something like... "Well Sarah, because I am so committed to your *results* and *satisfaction*, I want to tell you about a new training programme that's about to come on the market. It teaches in a really *fun* interactive way aimed at helping you get more *fulfilment* from life and work whilst increasing your ability to earn *money*. Sound interesting?"

Sometimes the voice isn't your own

With all this talk of inner voices you may be wondering how they got there in the first place. Do babies and toddlers have an inner voice? It's an interesting question and one that many a child expert would give differing answers to. I like the idea of small babies looking up at us from their crib and having a little chat to themselves about the funny faces and voices we pull... even if they don't currently have language skills. Although experts have mixed views, one thing I can share with certainty from personal experience is that some of your inner voices as an adult aren't your own. Someone else at some point in your life may have said something to you, often unintentionally, that stuck – it got inside your head. You may have constructed meaning from what they said and you've repeated it to yourself over and over again.

STORY

My experience of this led to me being in a career that really didn't suit me, play to my strengths or make me happy. For me, the voice was one that said, 'Get a proper job'. I now know that the voice wasn't my own but was my Dad's... and he had never, to my knowledge, ever actually said that to me! *(So Dad, when you're reading this, thanks for the great story and it wasn't you, I promise, it was me.)* Whilst I was growing up Dad was a telecoms engineer, and he was a great mathematician. Add to that my tendency towards being a tomboy rather than girlie as a child and you've got a period of formative years where I was desperate to do things that connected with Dad. So when it came to the time for me to choose which subjects I would study for my GCSEs, I took a really sensible view and went for sciences and maths, so that I could get a proper job, alongside French, because it looked like business in the future would be EU-driven, and as a back-up keyboard skills, so if all else failed I could become a secretary. Now as a 41 year-old, looking back on my decision-making as a 13 year-old, I'm not sure whether to laugh or cry. I'm impressed with the rational approach and horrified with the lack of emotional connection to any of the decisions. I love how things have turned out though, so I can be forgiving at the same time.

As a child and an adult, you have an inner need as a human being to be loved. Because of this basic human need, you make decisions from a really early age based on what is most likely to get love from those who are important to you in your life. Knowing this as an adult can change your life, if you take the time to stand back from your decisions and consider whose voice is driving the decision making.

Location, location, location – it's true for property but not for life

If you believe that where you come from or where you are today dictates where your future lies, then you'll make it true... even though it doesn't have to be. Holding onto that kind of belief can seriously damage the possibilities you allow yourself. Although we have huge brainpower compared to the common flea, we do seem to have a similar pattern when it comes to limiting ourselves. I once saw an experiment being done at the Natural History Museum to demonstrate some part of the evolutionary cycle using fleas and boxes with lids. A flea can jump an extraordinarily long way. Up to 200 times its body length! Imagine how long that would be for a human. If you have the flea in a tub and put the lid on, the flea may try to jump. Once it has hit against the lid a few times, you can safely take the lid off as the flea will no longer jump further than the height of the box where it had previously hit its head. As humans we are unlikely to have literally been held in a box and hit our heads, but metaphorically we limit our thinking and beliefs all the time. It may serve a purpose in terms of protecting us from imagined failure or ridicule, but it also means we only ever stay in the box we were born into or placed in: unless we make a conscious choice to jump out – which we can at any time. Your brain is much bigger than the flea's, so you have a choice!

STORY

....

A few years ago I was commissioned as career coach for a newly-appointed marketing director in a large insurance company in London. Andrew, the Marketing Director, had worked at the insurers for his whole career and was one of the youngest at the boardroom table. The CEO, John, was a real sponsor for Andrew and believed that he had what it takes to become his successor within the next 7/8 years, but there were some behavioural traits that would hold him back. Andrew had a tendency when at the board table to remain quiet, or when he did speak up it was in an apologetic fashion. Where he was presenting information, plans or successes from marketing, he was seen as too involved in the detail and lacking strategic vision. So we embarked on our coaching relationship with these as two of our areas of focus. As we explored them, both through conversation and observation, it became clear that Andrew didn't lack the ability to think strategically, rather it was about his confidence and beliefs. He had a story running in his mind that the only way, as a kid from a council estate, that he could add value with his elders was through technical knowledge. This drove him to include far too much data in his conversation and even in his presentation slides. Rather than thinking of his audience and what they needed to hear, he had been focussing on his own insecurities which drove the unhelpful behaviour. The work we did together unpicked some of his beliefs, and as he began to understand where they had come from, it was as if he was updating a much younger part of him that he'd 'done good', that he wasn't the same kid as in the 70s and 80s, and that the Andrew who sat around the table in 2012 belonged there.

What became really interesting, as I watched the changes happening for him, was the physiological shift. Seeing him enter the room, you now actually noticed him. It was as if he had grown taller in some way. John remained true to his beliefs about Andrew's potential, and he was promoted to an international directorship within six months of making the changes through our coaching work and was able to bring both his technical knowledge and his relaxed strategic vision to the fore...and enjoy it.

TIP:

When was the last time you updated yourself? Have a chat with your younger you and let him/her know how you're doing. Let him/her know that you've survived the teenage years, that you're now a parent, that your career is working out. Whatever it might be, let him/her know, and notice the relaxation that comes from it.

Peer groups matter

Studies since the 1950s including the Aasch experiment have shown us the power of group dynamics. Those with whom we spend time have a powerful impact on our behaviour and choices. In the Aasch experiment, a group of individuals is invited to a test environment. Only one is a 'real' person, with everyone else being actors set up as part of the experiment unbeknown to him. During the experiment they show a card with 4 lines drawn on it as shown below:

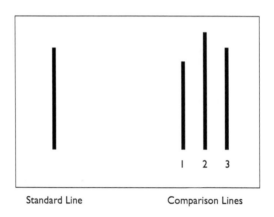

Standard Line   Comparison Lines

The actors have been told to choose line 1, not the one that is very obviously the same as the sample line in length. During the first round the 'real' subject states the correct line as being the same length, but incredibly quickly he acquiesces to the group's incorrect choice. It's worth watching on YouTube, not only to see the fabulous fashion of the time but also the confused look on the 'real' subject's face as he makes his decision about which line to pick.

Peer influence can be seen in every walk of life, from the marines at the top of their field, to 'X Factor' and other talent shows where 'the good, the bad and the ugly' try to follow their dream. In the talent show format, amongst those who are genuinely brilliant is a small but significant group which makes great viewing but is a worrying indictment of society and parenting today. They are often seen surrounded by family and friends who have been telling them for years how amazing their voice is… and as you watch, even before they enter the audition room, something tells you that they are about to screech like a cat at best and scream like a mating vixen at worst! Peer influence may give confidence in this scenario, and yet if it is not based on ability so the ultimate impact can only be flawed and damaging in the long term.

At the opposite end of the ability scale and peer-level feedback you've got the marines. During my days living just outside their Exmouth barracks I saw these impressive individuals and their influence both at work and at play. During one weekend conversation with an ex-marine, whilst travelling into Exeter on the train, I came to learn about what happens to many of them when they leave the service. They go from being among peers who are all driven, athletic and have high expectations of one another, to civilian home life where those around them are more likely to be accepting of the mediocrity of everyday life. This can cause depression at worst and many ex-marines end up falling well below average standards of living in their early years after leaving the service.

Proximity is power for the good and the bad.

EXERCISE

....

Peer audit

Now may be the time for you to do a review of those you have in your life. Are they there through choice, habit or convenience? Do they reflect the life you want to live? Are they in support of you or do they take more than give? Difficult questions to answer and sometimes you may choose to keep someone in your life because they are family or it would cross an ethical line for you to cut them off. That's okay as long as you do it knowingly.

1. Make a list of all the people you currently spend time with.

2. Consider when they came into your life:

    a. What were you doing then?

    b. What kind of person were you back then?

    c. What has made you remain connected?

3. Consider your relationship today:

    a. Do they have a positive impact on your life?

    b. Are they a peer that you admire in some way or that is reflective of the kind of life that you want to live?

    c. If they were no longer part of your life what impact would it have? What would then be possible/not possible?

4. Having mapped out your current peer group add in where you think there may be gaps:

    a. Where would you like to have more peers? E.g. creative people, people with drive, parents.....

5. Decide what shape your peer group should be and who you would like to be in it in 12 months' time.

6. Act – do something to make the change... ... ...

....

Belief drives reality – what you believe you create

Reality is such an interesting word. Is it a concept? Is it what is? Is it important? What does it mean to and for you? Our beliefs are intrinsically attached to our values, those things in our lives that are of most importance. So you might think that they can't change so why worry - but you can change if you choose to. Things change in terms of importance, or our understanding of things changes through time and experience. Life is not static by nature even for those of us with a love for keeping things the same. It would save me a fortune if hair didn't go grey and lots of energy if it was as easy at 40 as at 30 to stay a certain dress size!

> *"If you don't change your beliefs, your life will be like this forever. Is that good news?"*
>
> W. Somerset Maugham

Change your thinking, change your reality

It seems to be becoming endemic in the UK culture to focus externally when things don't go our way. Fall over a loose paving slab and rather than thinking 'I really must look where I'm going' it seems many think first that 'the council should have fixed that'. Don't get a promotion and some think it's about the interviewer or the bias in the system rather than asking what they could have done differently, or accepting that they were just not a good fit for the role. It may be that the externally focussed thoughts are correct but to think them and believe them to be reality can be paralysing and depressing.

Thinking creatively around problems that emerge can offer greater options and success by keeping you focussed on what you want. Whatever you are focussed upon you'll get drawn towards, so if you maintain focus on the problem then the likelihood is that you'll get more of the same, or certainly fail to break out of the current situation. You may even try approaches to changing the situation that have worked previously, but find this time there's no progress. Do you keep doing the same but try harder when this happens or do you change your approach? I'd suggest a change of approach is more likely to be fruitful, especially if you remember the old adage of the definition of madness – doing the same thing and expecting a different result!

> *"We can't solve problems by using the same kind of thinking we used when we created them."*
>
> *Albert Einstein*

Solution-focussed thinking is something that can work for you as an individual and it can have amazing results at an organisational level.

STORY

Working with a global manufacturing company I was told a story of some issues that they were having in their Italian manufacturing plant. It was related to the Health and Safety Executive's equivalent in Europe and HR disciplinary processes, so I introduced them to a colleague who was highly experienced in the field (Adele). Once Adele researched the issue it became apparent that although the stated problem was that the factory was under notice of potential shutdown due to safety breaches, the root of the issue was influencing the shop floor team to wear their safety goggles. The HR team and management had tried traditional ways to change their behaviour such as written warnings and more informal requests, but to no avail. Adele and I put our heads together and talked about using the solution-focussed approach because it takes into account more creative ways of thinking and gets you out of your own way.

EXERCISE

....

Solution-focused approach

Take yourself through the steps below with a problem that you currently want to change either at work or home. It doesn't have to be huge, it can be an everyday problem, but do make sure it's one that matters to you. Notice how it feels different and what impact that has on your resourcefulness.

Step 1 – Define what's the problem.

> *In Adele's Italian example it was the potential factory shut down due to the team not wearing safety equipment.*

Step 2 – Define what you want. If you were to wake up tomorrow morning and the problem had disappeared what would be the first indicators to you that things had changed?

> *In the Italian example it was that the safety notice would be lifted and all the shop floor team would be happily wearing their safety equipment, including goggles.*

Step 3 – Where else in the world does what you describe in step 2 already exist to some degree?

> *In our example in Italy, men (who made up 99% of the shop floor team) wore glasses happily when out in the sunshine – sun glasses!*

Step 4 – Apply the thinking to your current situation.

> *In Italy the management invested with a designer from Prada to create new-look goggles for the shop floor team. Still safety-focussed but looking good and designer branded…job done!*

You won't be wrong – as a human it's in your DNA

There's something peculiar in all of us as human beings on this planet that may manifest itself in different ways but at its root has the same driver. It's the survival instinct, the drive to not be wrong. It's not the 'I'm right at all costs' version that I'm referring to, it's the need to feel validated. For some of us we may come at it through arguing our point but for others it can be a sense of quiet knowing and not engaging. In organisations you get a sense of their level of sophistication around the topic by noticing the language they use and the levels of creativity that are allowed or encouraged. When I'm working within organisations I keep my ears open to hearing general conversation around the offices and sites so that I get a feel for the culture in terms of openness. If I hear a lot of 'Yes but' then I can often safely hypothesise that there is a certain defensiveness inbuilt in the culture and if I hear 'Yes and' then often we can make progress at speed because it is in the nature of the environment to listen and then suggest rather than prove a point. 'Yes buts' breed return volleys of 'Yes buts' and take you down a rather narrow conversational alleyway that can only lead to one of you being right and the other having to back down in some way. You'll even hear this style of conversation in your personal life. Recently I was listening to friends discussing their holiday plans for this year. It went a little like this:

Mark: "This year I'd love to go trekking again, maybe in Mexico."

Fiona: "Yes but we've already done the trekking thing so can't we do something different this time?"

Mark: "Yes but I love the exercise and the adventurous

way we can explore with trekking. We get to see the real country rather than the tourist bit."

Fiona: "Yes but in Mexico it's not really safe and I've been working really hard lately and just want to relax."

Mark: "Yes but it's so boring going on a beach holiday. You know I don't like just sitting around."

Fiona and Mark continued like this for a rather long time and were seemingly getting nowhere. They've still not booked a holiday as it's still under discussion.

If they had taken the 'Yes and' approach, maybe it could have gone somewhat differently:

Mark: "This year I'd love to go trekking again, maybe in Mexico."

Fiona: "Yes and I know how much you love it although I've been working really hard lately and was hoping to relax more this year."

Mark: "Yes and relaxing sounds good although I do get bored on those beach holidays so I would probably drive you crazy."

Fiona: "Yes and maybe we could find an option that includes activities but is based in a resort?"

Mark: "Yes and if we can find one that isn't too mainstream that would be good because you know how I hate the whole touristy thing."

Fiona: "Yes and I agree so let's get some brochures and have a look online at options."

Try it out for a while and see what a difference in makes to your own conversations.

One thing I consistently notice is that when you run through the two different approaches, 'Yes and' opens up options whereas 'Yes but' closes you down. Feeling closed down is often what creates defensive behaviour in most of us and can cause us to feel unheard and so get louder. The act of feeling defensive is coupled with a focal vision that closes our physicality inward which, if you try it on for size, is not the best frame to be in to think creatively or to open up new possibilities or solutions.

A sense of being judged may be something that you find affects you. I notice that it's a common trigger for clients that I work with, and from personal experience both inside and outside of work it has its impact. I am eternally grateful for the work I did personally around my reaction to feeling judged because any of you with small children in your lives will know the power of judgment that can come from others when you are out and about and a tantrum occurs.

When we think about judgment, there is a single word that I notice creates an immediate, and yet subtle, reaction in most people... the word 'why'. If someone asks you, "Where do you live?" followed by, "What made you choose that area?" or, "What specifically was it you liked about that area?", you are likely to respond in quite an open and relaxed way because it feels that they are interested and curious. If the same person were to ask, "Where do you live?" and then follow up with, "Why did you choose that area?" or, "Why there?", it has a sense of, "I'm judging your choice about it" and, for some, this can put you on the defensive about either your choices or the area you live in. 'Why?' is a powerful question and used in negotiations can be incredibly useful, so keep it in your toolkit, although you may want to consider when and with whom you use it. It may not be helpful in achieving your outcomes!

TIP:

Try switching the word 'why' for 'what/who/how/where specifically' next time you're asking a question, and notice the different types of response you get.

So, having touched on some language that may frame our reactions and beliefs, let's look at our opinions. You are most likely to believe that the opinions or generalisations that you hold are true. They are held not only in your mind but also at a muscular level, and this is because when you first formed your opinion on something you would have had a physiological reaction as well as a psychological one. Your brain and your body react and remember. You experience a need to defend an opinion in your body because it happens at an unconscious level. Then your brain gets involved and begins to rationalise and look for justifications and counter arguments to begin to restore some balance and a sense of 'rightness'. It's a totally healthy reaction and one that you can encourage and practice by testing out new or contradictory ideas. In most cases you will find that you can cope with a little discomfort and can change your mind if better or new information comes to light that offers a different perspective. This may not be true for you if the person/source that is offering the new information is in any way scary, or if you feel vulnerable or where there is a lot of risk involved. Knowing this can be incredibly helpful when helping others to make healthy choices, as you can create a safe environment for them to explore their thinking. It can, of course, also make the difference for you in how decisive you feel you are able to be. If you get stuck on a choice, it may be because you are holding your opinion too tightly or that you have gone into defensive mode because it feels unsafe in some way. Knowing this means you can change it. You need to ensure that your relationship with yourself is a healthy one so that you can feel able to experiment and grow. Those who are able to challenge and grow in our constantly changing world, both in business and life generally, are the ones who remain vital and manage the demands so as to make a contribution.

EXERCISE

. . . .

Opinions

Having opinions is no bad thing. They are inevitable in life and can make things interesting – as long as you acknowledge them as opinions rather than truths.

Take some time to consider the statements below. Notice first your initial gut reaction, and then play with the possibilities of how you might challenge and argue from each possible standpoint on them.

Where do you stand on the following beliefs?

Every behaviour has a positive intention

There is no such thing as a wrong decision

Everyone has the right to be happy

Everyone's worldview is equally true and equally valid

Everyone has what it takes to create success

We are all part of the same system

No one ever learns by being made wrong

The measure of communication is the response it gets

What did you notice as you read the statements of opinion? Did you have a different reaction to those you agreed with and those you didn't? Are you already beginning to consider that there could be other views?

For those that you had a negative reaction to, consider what might be behind it and what would need to be true for someone to hold the opinion in the first place.

Being able to hold an opinion and be open to others' views can lead to a much more effective leadership style or way to live your life.

Feeling overwhelmed is an indicator of your inner drive

Inner drive is something that most of you may take for granted or not really have thought about before. It's the thing that gets us out of bed, that gets us working, that makes things happen in our lives. Without drive you are stranded, stuck in the place that you find yourself. Being overwhelmed is often an indicator that we may be overusing our drive. Like any strength, if overused, it becomes our weakness. For example, being focussed is a strength, but being overly focussed can be limiting as you may miss opportunities that arise simply because you don't see them. Being kind, if overdone, can turn into being sycophantic or becoming a doormat.

Without inner drive we would never do / achieve / challenge anything

Wanting to achieve can be an amazing driver. It can motivate you to get to heights that you had never considered possible. Those of you with an achiever motivation will enjoy ticking things off your list as they get done. You'll have a list whether it's the weekend or a workday. The list may not be written down, it may be in your mind, but it exists. It'll probably be much longer than the time available too. You may have this inner flame naturally, or you may find that you are drawn to people whom you consider self-starters. Either way, the drive of the achiever gets stuff done. If overused though, this form of inner drive becomes overwhelming or turns into self-flagellation. If the list gets too long or at the end of each day there's no acknowledgement of what you have achieved, you may feel demotivated and frustrated. If the list doesn't recalibrate to zero and then carry forward, you may find yourself feeling overwhelmed.

Consider this in terms of your career, and it can build every day as you head to work, the sense of needing to do more than is possible and it all needing to be done today. Add to that family pressures, desires to learn and grow, the everyday hygiene factor, mundane tasks that have to happen, and things get pretty full if we focus too closely and see them all at once.

When looking to build a business or launch a product on the market, planning is key. You'll map out the phases and stages that are required from resources, such as the people and skills needed, through to the branding and communication elements. Often when working as a career coach with individuals, it strikes me that the approach being taken to building a career can mirror that of any product. After all, a career is a series of jobs, and jobs are a trade of your time and skills for money... so you are providing a product.

STORY

During a coaching session with a senior marketing manager at a telecoms company we got to talking about future aspirations in this way. Chris had taken a structured approach to developing his career so far, but he was hitting a barrier as the structure he had been using was too inflexible. He had reached an age where he wanted to start a family and also, being in his early 30s, felt that this was the time to really push to achieve success in career terms. We applied the 'Me Plc' approach to mapping out his next career/life choices, and the sense of being overwhelmed that Chris had previously felt dissipated as it provided him with clarity of steps for action going forward.

EXERCISE

....

ME Plc

In today's job market you need to stand out to get on. One way of doing that is to consider yourself the CEO of your own company and your skills are your products. If you were the CEO of company ME Plc, what might you do differently? There are a number of aspects to take into account, so consider the following questions:

- Who do you want on your board of directors? (mentors, coaches, supporters and challengers)

- What knowledge do you have, and how might you play to your strengths or shore up weaknesses and gaps in knowledge?

- What exactly is your product? Who do you anticipate buying your services? How will you find them? How will you approach them? What is the competition and what can they 'do' for you?

- How much do you need/want to earn? What's your attitude to risk? What do you want your cash flow and forecasting for the next few years to look like?

- What kind of lifestyle do you want to create?

....

Spring cleaning is the answer

Being overwhelmed can come as a result of many triggers, and yet the result of it has a consistent feeling – the feeling of temporary paralysis. That sense that the job is so big that all you can think is OMG! This sensation is often created when there is too much to do or you've too much at the front of your mind with no clear place to start. It is becoming a more common feeling these days, maybe because never before have we had so many choices or so much information available to us in any moment. Go back just 20 years, and to research a particular company or to understand a market place or topic area, you would have had to head to the library or Companies House. Discussions were based on things we'd learnt previously or remembered, whereas today a question arises and we look to our Smartphone or tablet, and a simple Google search provides the answers.

The ability to be able to view the world from our armchair has also led to a raised awareness of what is possible; all good things in that they provide greater choice, and yet with choice comes responsibility. With responsibility can come a fear of failure or choosing the wrong path. You might even think that you need to be able to do it all. Personally, I would never want to go back in time to being a woman in a world where your only choice was about what to cook for dinner, a time that my Mother grew up in, when you were lucky to be able to choose who to marry and that your career was to be a wife and mother, no matter how well educated you may have been. I'm grateful to have the choice to be a career woman as well as a wife and mother, although the pressure that comes with attempting to 'do it all' does come at a price. For me it's one of the reasons why being able to manage those moments in life that feel overwhelming is of utmost importance in 2013 and beyond.

If learning to manage feelings of being overwhelmed is something that you would find useful, then practice the exercise below.

EXERCISE

....

A mental spring clean

Like any skill, training and practice are key to building the muscle and embedding the learning, so allow yourself to imagine the scenario and feel the changes as you walk through the steps.

1. Find yourself an environment that for you feels comfortable. Somewhere you are happy to close your eyes and imagine…

2. Now close your eyes and imagine you are walking through your front door at home. It's the time of year when the daffodils are nodding their golden heads outside and the light that streams through your windows is the kind that makes you smile and at the same time highlights that it's time to spring clean! With the warmth of the sun on your back as you walk through your home, you begin to make a mental list of all the areas that you need to sort out. As you list them, you hold them all front of mind in order to make sure you remember…

   … walk into your kitchen. The cupboards need reorganising, those tins that have been at the back of the cupboard need checking for dates, and then the inside of the cupboard needs cleaning before you put them back. Under the cabinets you'll need to get to the back, and the oven, then the fridge and the tiles...

... next go into your bedroom, and there's the wardrobe and drawers to sort through and clear out the clothes that you've not worn for so long, those that need repairing, odd socks to sort and throw out, get under the bed to have a good clean and see how much has been pushed under throughout the winter...

... now into the bathroom and the bathroom cabinet. Disposing of anything out of date, making sure that old products are cleared away. The back of the U bend and behind the sink and cistern, the grout and the tiles, cleaning the mirror, the top of the cupboard, sorting through the towels...

3. As you imagined, in each of the areas of your home that needed sorting through there would likely have come a point where it began to feel overwhelming (unless you're like my good friend Jo who lives in a perfect show home all year round). The point of feeling overwhelmed is different for all of us, and the point to stop and take a breath needs to be taken wherever you feel the overwhelm beginning.

4. The point of being overwhelmed is the time to begin to chunk things down. So first imagine in front of you that instead of all the rooms being held in one space, you push (in your mind's eye) the kitchen to your left, your bathroom to the right, and leave the bedroom in front of you. You now have an order of rooms to begin working through.

a. Let's break it down further. Start with the kitchen, so look to your left where you moved it a moment ago and now pull it towards you, making the other rooms move further back in your imagination. Separate each of the areas that need sorting in the same way as you did with the rooms. Push the cupboards to the left, under the cabinets to the right and the oven stays in front of you.

b. Let's break it down even further. Take the kitchen cupboards from the left where you placed them a moment ago and move them in front of you, which again moves the other areas further away. Now, with the cupboards let's decide which order to start the sorting. Food cupboard first, then the crockery.

5. Get started – empty out all the food from the cupboard and get cleaning just that one. Know that you have a mental or written list of the rest and will get to it all in good time. One step at a time over a period of time...

Notice how it feels different to have each area separated on your own line of time. Each task individual and achievable, one task at a time.

Comfort is the killer of change

Change only ever occurs in your life when something becomes too painful, or you are drawn to something compelling and pleasurable. It's part of the human condition to stay in comfort until you must change. How many times have you heard someone say, 'I can't believe where the last x number of years have gone and I'm still at the company. I'd only planned to be here a couple of years!' When I'm career coaching it's something I hear often, and in these times of economic uncertainty it seems to have become even more common. Maybe because the desire for comfort and certainty has grown and change feels more risky than it may have done in a more buoyant job market.

> *"Move out of your comfort zone. You can only grow if you are willing to feel awkward and uncomfortable when you try something new."*
>
> *Brian Tracy*

There have been many studies over the years about change and human behaviour. All the studies come from differing perspectives and all have some nuggets of wisdom that you can use. One of the nuggets that I find useful is the knowledge and awareness that unless a 'must' or a 'need' is present, then the likelihood of you making a change is minimal. This has been shown to be true in my own life as much as when I am in the role of coach. As soon as I hear "I'm trying to...", "I should..." or, "I'd like to..." then I know that something is missing to make it compelling enough for you to change. It may be that you've been told that something needs to change rather than you actually wanting it. Societal pressures or more direct instruction from a boss can lead to a stated desire for change. These are not enough, though. There has to be a consequence to making the change for you personally that is far enough up or down the scale of good/bad to make you feel it is a must to have change.

BAD ⟶ COMFORT ⟶ GOOD
(pain) (pleasure)

STORY

In seven years of working as an executive coach I will have worked with hundreds of people for thousands of hours, and in all this time I have only actively disengaged and pulled the plug on a couple of contracts. Each time this was due to it becoming apparent that the individual didn't actually want the change stated in their objectives for the coaching work. On one such occasion I was working with Den, an engineering director for a global building company. Den had returned from a role as country MD for one of the group's companies in the Middle East and had worked for the organisation for nearly 30 years. Coming back to the UK he was appointed to a corporate board role and was finding the transition difficult. His leadership style was autocratic and alpha male, and this was having a demotivating impact on the team of highly qualified professionals that Den was now managing. The HR Director and the CEO of the company were both actively involved in wanting Den to succeed and had been part of the objective-setting exercise as well as having provided detailed feedback on what they observed and felt needed flexing in behavioural terms. Den turned up for our meetings and during the sessions engaged in the conversations as well as committing to actions back in the office... but nothing seemed to move forward which got me curious. After some digging I learned that although each of the parties that were stakeholders in wanting the change were rationally engaged, there was no consequence to any change being made, either positive or negative. If Den stayed working in his current style, then nothing happened to his detriment, and if he was seen to flex his behaviour, then there was no reward. So standing in Den's shoes – why would you make the effort to change?

What is comfort stopping you from doing? If anything were possible for you, what would you change?

CHAPTER 5

The Time Is Now – Let's Do It

Let's get cracking! Make your choices and then do something. Anything. If you want things to be different, even in a small way, you need to take action. There's a time for standing back, for contemplating, and there's a time for doing. Once you've made your choice, get moving and take action. Make something happen, get creating.

Nothing ever happened without energy

Energy is the difference between being alive and being dead. Simple, really, to choose between those options! If you look back over your time, you'll notice that any choice you have made will have been followed by action. Even if that action was to stand still. Actions come in many shapes, sizes, speeds and intensities. One thing your examples will all have in common is that to take them you would have needed clarity and belief. In the moment of action you would have known what you were doing and believed that you could do it. Whether it wavered or grew once you'd started to act is a separate thing – that's about maintaining energy and momentum, not getting started. You know how to get started, you'll have done it every day, many times over, unless you are sitting in the same spot day after day not doing anything.

Know your style and how to maintain it

To make a change you need to know a couple of things about your energy. How to tap into it and how to maintain it. To help you with that, it can be useful to understand your energetic style.

STORY

When I was living in the New Forest and working for B&Q at their head office in Chandler's Ford, I learned that the difference in these preferences were at the heart of my failure to be able to manage the pressure I was under and my energy levels. I knew that what I needed was some headspace, some thinking time, to be able to step back and be more strategic, and yet the volume of what needed to be achieved drove me into action constantly. I set myself goals to read business articles, booked time in my calendar to take myself off by myself away from my desk to 'think', and I believed that quiet time on my own was the answer. Time after time I would begin well but then fall over around the third or fourth week. My energy to sustain the change in behaviour would lapse. Anyone who has ever met me would be able to tell you that I am someone who loves people. Someone who gets energised in groups and who generates energy with others rather than alone. This realisation got me thinking as to my approach to creating headspace. Maybe what I needed was to play to my strength to create the headspace? So I tested it. Between where I lived and the office was a gym. I knew this because often I'd be sitting in traffic on the M271 of an evening right next to it. So I joined, and rather than sitting in the car, I would spend an hour or so every evening on the static bikes or the treadmill, and think. I was surrounded by people but not engaging with them, so my energy kept high throughout and I got the quiet time in my head that I needed to be able to step back and think broadly. An added benefit was that I was fitter then than I have ever been. Headspace and contemplation doesn't have to be done in a quiet environment or even sitting still.

EXERCISE

....

Your energy preference

The preferences around energy that were at the heart of my story have been highlighted by a number of psychologists over the years. The one that makes a lot of sense for me and has clarity was developed back in the 1950s by a mother and daughter-in-law who wanted to create a tool that looked at personality preferences based on Jungian psychology and was accessible to all. A tool that, although you need to qualify to use it, can be understood by non-psychologists and can be used in a day-to-day way to make a difference to your life. One of the dichotomies that the Myers Briggs Type Indicator looks at is the one that tells us where we get our energy from, which is key when considering how we make choices and the energy we have to make them.

As you read the descriptors I'll share below, it's good to keep in mind a couple of things:

1. The language is rather stuck in the 50s when words had different meanings – just think of words like merry and gay and you'll get what I mean. The 21st century meaning is a little different. So introversion doesn't mean shy, for instance.

2. We are multi-faceted as human beings and so you may find that you do a little of both. Like being right or left-handed though, it is likely that you will have a preference for one over the other.

3. Neither preference is a measure of competence – they are about our energy – again like handwriting, you can be right-handed and have really bad handwriting.

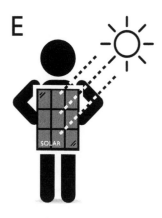

Extroversion

The natural focus of extraversion
is the external world

Introversion

The natural focus of introversion
is the internal world

Here are some words that may help you identify your preference:

Extraversion	Introversion
• Attuned to external environment	• Drawn to their inner world
• Prefer to communicate by talking	• Prefer to communicate in writing
• Work out ideas by talking them through	• Work out ideas by reflecting on them
• Learn best through doing or discussing	• Learn best by reflection, mental 'practice'
• Have broad interests	• Focus in depth on their interests
• Sociable and expressive	• Private and contained
• Readily take initiative in work and relationships	• Take initiative when the situation or issue is very important to them

Introduction to Type by Isabel Briggs Myers published by OPP

Which is more like you?

Which do you have a greater affinity with?

Once you know your preference, you can choose environments and activities that play to what works naturally for you. There's little merit in practicing writing with your left hand if you're right-handed if you want your handwriting to be better, so when it comes to managing your energy it makes sense to practice in a way that comes naturally. You'll get better results and faster.

Knowing your energetic type also means that you have a fast track to understanding and managing the stressors that will affect your energy. It means that you can make choices in life that help you manage your energy better.

EXERCISE

....

Working with stressors for different 'types'

Typical work stressors for each 'type':

Stressors for extraverts	Stressors for introverts
• Working alone • Having to communicate mainly by email • Lengthy work periods with no interruptions • Having to reflect before taking action • Having to focus in depth on one thing • Getting feedback in writing only	• Working with others • Talking on the phone a lot • Interacting with others frequently • Having to act quickly without reflection • Too many concurrent tasks and demands • Getting frequent and verbal feedback

If any of these stressors seem familiar to you ask yourself the following questions:

1. How much does your current circumstance/job play to your preference?

2. What might you do to better match your needs and avoid the stressors?

Coping with being different

Most of us don't get the opportunity to choose the people we spend our time with at work. Even where you are the boss and get to recruit your team you most likely need to bring in people with a mix of skills and personalities to ensure the job gets done. This means that having strategies in place to cope with being different from your team can pay dividends.

Where you find yourself working in an environment where most others have the opposite energetic 'type', these tactics may help mitigate the effects:

If you prefer extraversion and your team/workgroup are mostly introverted have a go at some of the following suggestions:

- Network with people outside of your team or organisation

- Ask other people to share their ideas with you in conversation

- Pay attention to written notices and email

- Allow other people to think about your idea for a while before they need to provide feedback (count to 10 if you need to)

If you prefer introversion and your team/workgroup are mostly extraverted have a go at some of the following suggestions:

- Arrive at work earlier than your colleagues to take advantage of the peace and quiet

- Intentionally seeking out private/reflective time throughout the day

- Take the long way home

- In meetings, practise voicing partially thought-through perspectives

Managing your energy well doesn't mean becoming a yogi and spending days recouping. A little rest and relaxation can be a lovely thing and can help you maintain health but, depending on your energetic style, what R&R looks like for you will be very different. For some, white water rafting creates inner peace much more than any yoga class may!

> *"People who cannot find time for recreation are obliged sooner or later to find time for illness."*
>
> *John Wanamaker*

Energy is power

In both a literal and a metaphorical sense energy is power. Whether you think of the kind of energy that comes from the National Grid and power stations or the more personal power that you exude, they both have movement to them. That movement doesn't need to be fast to win through, although in today's world that may not feel like the truth.

Remember the story of the tortoise and the hare?

Once upon a time a hare met a tortoise whilst walking very slowly towards the market one Sunday. The hare was proud of how fast he was and so made fun of the slow tortoise. But the tortoise was good-natured and replied, "I may have short legs and small feet, but I can beat you in a race." The proud hare laughed and said, "I can beat you within a second!" So he readily agreed to the race knowing that he would be able to win.

The next day Alf the elephant, who was the judge of the jungle, began the race by shouting, "Get! Set! Go!" The other animals waited at the finish line near the marketplace whilst some cheered on the tortoise along the route.

When the hare had covered half of the distance he looked back and saw the tortoise far, far behind. The hare thought, "Let me take a nap. I can run fast and easily win this race!" He sat under a tree and dozed off. When the tortoise passed, he found the hare sleeping and quietly smiled to himself as he walked on by.

The hare woke up and realised that the race was already over. He'd missed the tortoise walking by and his chance to claim the race as the winner. The tortoise had reached the end and won the race! The hare was tripped up by his false sense of pride and defeated by determination and hard work.

Now does that mean that sometimes the hare wouldn't win? I imagine not. If the race was over 100 metres then arguably speed off the start line would matter. But knowing which kind of power and energy you need in your own context is a key ingredient to success. In business there will inevitably be times when speed is required and other times when a more constant considered pace may be favourable. When did you last experience the steady version, though?

Speed can often negate the key leadership quality of being present and available to others. You may find that it cannot be practiced if you are racing along like the hare. Would you even notice other people around you?

TIP:

Consider your context – What's the optimum speed for the task at hand?

STORY

Kath, a Strategy Director, had been working like the hare and achieving a lot in a business context. Even with the successes in her role she found that she wasn't satisfied either at home or work. Kath didn't feel as if she was making any progress towards her goal of becoming an MD and she felt she was missing out on her children's early years because of her long commute. It wasn't until she slowed down and consciously chose to move out of London, so that she could be at home more (not difficult, given her commute had been four hours a day), that she achieved her goal of becoming MD almost as a by-product of being more fulfilled at home and able to focus. Slowing down her pace paid dividends!

Know your style of delivery and work WITH it!

Why, oh why, do so many people believe that the way to succeed is to act like other people? Emulating the traits and behaviours of others you admire is a fabulous way of learning and growing – but only if you do it as you, and not by trying to become them. It's great to understand and value different approaches and ways of working. Borrow them, even steal them with pride, if they work and it doesn't hurt the original owner.

Work with your natural style rather than attempting to play to your flaws or attempting to become someone else. I'm speaking from personal experience having worked in finance for so many years and qualifying as an auditor at a military school (where I was the only civilian). Looking back, the clue that I wasn't playing to my natural talents was that I learned most of the facts in the accountancy paper by creating poetry to remember what was on each line of the books. Let's just say my creative mind was screaming at me for choosing a profession that relied so heavily on my analytical brain.

Working against my natural style was okay, I made it work and did pretty well, but it was incredibly tiring and frustrating. When I was out in the field conducting an audit I rarely got my successes through pure analysis. I moulded the job so that I got results by building relationships with the management teams, and they told me where the flaws and problems were so I could investigate and suggest ways of improving. Not your average approach in the profession I can assure you.

Go against your natural style and you may fail to maintain change

Often I find myself bringing a new perspective to old conversations. One is around prioritisation and managing your time. Time management as a label is flawed in my opinion. You cannot manage time. There are 60 minutes in every hour, 24 hours in a day and 365 days in a year, and that means that we all have the same amount of time to use and can't do anything to change that. What we can change though is the choices we make on how we use the time. You will have your own personal style when it comes to how you choose to use the time you have, and your life experiences will have affected it along the way. Speaking at a national convention, I was privileged to have someone alongside me who shared her personal story about how time feels different to her since she was diagnosed with inoperable cancer. As a young mum with a flourishing career, she shared how her 'bucket list' is now incredibly focussed. She had real clarity on what is important to her and for her, and at the top of that list is knowing that by the time she leaves this mortal earth she has made a difference. Now most of us, hopefully, will not have such a life-changing thing happen to us and yet we can certainly learn from her experience.

Making the most of your time, and using it in a way that plays to how you think about it, is key to sustaining any change and therefore making sure you fit in the important things. Do you know how you're naturally wired to manage time?

EXERCISE

....

Time, a self-audit

Doing a self-audit of how you use your time can prove incredibly useful, and it's fast to do.

Grab a piece of paper and first list all the things you love to do, even those that you may not get to do often or at all.

Next make a list of all the things you've done over the past week. Remember to include sleeping, shopping, cooking food and all the mundane day-to-day stuff.

Once you have the list of what you have done, write next to each thing roughly how long you spent doing it. It doesn't have to be perfect, just a best guess.

Now add up the hours. How many do you have?

When I do this exercise at the beginning of time management workshops, it's interesting that often there will be a group of people who are shocked when I say that the number of hours there are in a week is 168 because they had added up their hours to a much larger number. There is another group who often breathe a sigh of relief when they find that their number of hours is much lower and so realise that they do have more time to play with than they may have thought.

....

Another way of considering time and prioritisation is using the Jungian-based psychometric I talked about earlier in this book, the Myers Briggs Type Indicator. The fourth dichotomy it describes has a massive impact on how we go about living our lives and has a particular impact on our use of time. Have a look at the descriptors below and get a sense of which you think may be more you. Remember that it's like 'handedness', in that you are left or right-handed and have the ability to use your least preferred hand should you need to. So neither is right or wrong, and whichever is your preference, it doesn't determine whether you'll be any good at it – just like handwriting.

Judging	Perceiving
• Scheduled	• Spontaneous
• Organise their lives	• Flexible
• Systematic	• Casual
• Methodical	• Open ended
• Make short and long-term plans	• Adapt, change course
• Like to have things decided	• Like things loose and open to change
• Try to avoid last minute stresses	• Feel energised by last minute pressures

Introduction to Type by Isabel Briggs Myers published by OPP

When I'm describing these preferences to clients I often think about out-of-work examples because, at work, we are often swayed and influenced by the culture of the company and the style of our boss. Think about how you might approach a trip to the cinema with friends.

If you are someone with a 'J' (Judging) preference, then you are likely to enjoy taking a methodical approach to organising the outing. You're likely to break down the task in a systematic way, starting as early as possible, even months before the event. You'll order tickets for collection at the cinema, book a table at the restaurant close by that guarantees a fast turnaround, email everyone details and share parking or transport link information... and enjoy every moment of it as it gets completed. You will like to have things decided as soon as it's agreed that you are all going out for the night, so that you can relax.

J

Interestingly, if you are someone with a 'P' (Perceiving) preference, you have probably just read this description of the approach to going to the cinema and found yourself cringing, pulling faces, and maybe even thinking "OMG, really!" For those of you with a 'P' way of being, the idea of getting things booked so early adds stress as it may feel like you could miss out on an opportunity for something better when the time comes. You like to keep your options open as long as is possible until you feel the pressure of the deadline. There could be a new restaurant open between now and when you go and you'd miss the chance to go if tickets are booked. You feel the energy to complete a task close to the deadline and enjoy the last-minute pressures, as they are what makes things fun and ensure the quality is the best it can be. It allows you to take a flexible approach depending on circumstances. You may also, if you've not accepted this as a preference, have labelled it as a weakness. You may look at your 'J' colleagues with envy, and saying lots of 'shoulds' to yourself, guilt-tripping with statements like, "I should start things earlier", "I should be more organised"…

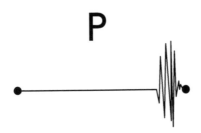

Imagine for a moment that you are working with, or even living with, someone with the opposite way of working. It can be really stressful for all concerned if you don't understand that these are both valid ways of working, and that the person with the different style isn't doing it to wind you up! Often I have observed that people with 'P' styles were sent on time management courses so that they could be straightened out… often sent by 'J' bosses. They would go to the course and learn some 'J'-type techniques, come back to the office and manage for a couple of weeks and then revert to type, much to the frustration and disappointment of all concerned. This inspired me to create a programme that teaches how to manage your time based on both the knowledge that it's about choice and also that there are many ways of doing it effectively.

TIPS FOR 'J's:

planning and prioritising; building in flexibility to your often rigid plans and ruthlessly prioritising the really important things – avoid the over-tasking that you may fall prey to.

TIPS FOR 'P's:

....

*deadlines, deadlines, deadlines – preferably involving other
people or some similarly immoveable demand.*

Whatever your type, the story below of the rocks and the sand
remains true in life.

> A philosophy professor stood before his class with
> some items on the table in front of him. When the
> class began, wordlessly he picked up a very large
> and empty mayonnaise jar and proceeded to fill it
> with rocks, each about 2 inches in diameter.
>
> He then asked the students if the jar was full. They
> agreed that it was.
>
> So the professor then picked up a box of pebbles and
> poured them into the jar. He shook the jar lightly.
> The pebbles, of course, rolled into the open areas
> between the rocks.
>
> He then asked the students again if the jar was full.
> They agreed it was.
>
> The professor picked up a box of sand and poured
> it into the jar. Of course, the sand filled up the
> remaining spaces in the jar.
>
> He then asked once more if the jar was full. The
> students responded with a unanimous, "Yes."

"Now," said the professor, "I want you to recognise that this jar represents your life. The rocks are the important things – your family, your partner, your health, your children – things that if everything else was lost and only they remained, your life would still be full. The pebbles are the other things that matter – like your job, your house, your car. The sand is everything else, the small stuff."

"If you put the sand into the jar first," he continued, "there is no room for the pebbles or the rocks. The same goes for your life. If you spend all your time and energy on the small stuff, you will never have room for the things that are important to you. Pay attention to the things that are critical to your happiness. Play with your children. Take your partner out dancing. There will always be time to go to work, clean the house, give a dinner party, or fix the waste disposal."

"Take care of the rocks first – the things that really matter. Set your priorities. The rest is just sand."

Author Unknown

Start up, maintenance, growth or turnaround?

Knowing your own style is important, not only to play to your strengths but also to be able to match your style to the situation or strategy of a company. Organisations are living entities in their own right and, as such, mature over time and are affected by internal and external forces.

If you are someone who operates at your best when there is a blank sheet of paper and you get to be creative about your approach, then being in an organisation that is in a consolidation or maintenance phase probably is not a good match for you.

When I'm coaching senior managers and especially CEOs, it has become as important to consider the longevity of role and the exit plan on appointment as it is to create a strategic plan to deliver what's needed today. Tenures for CEOs have dropped to below two years and this may be in part because fast results are required and so style match is much more transparent these days.

If you are someone who is really good at holding steady to the reins and making sure that things are maintained for the long-haul, then being in an organisation that requires radical change due to market forces is probably not where you will succeed. An example of this can be seen in the water companies in the UK. The market is due to be deregulated in 2017 and this will bring with it a need for greater dynamism and a more entrepreneurial approach to be able to grasp the opportunities that come with a broadened marketplace. If you don't think in that way and you maintain things as they have always been done because it has always worked, then the likelihood is that your competitors will take you out. This mismatching of style to business situation occurs more regularly than you may think.

STORY

....

Whilst working with a team in a manufacturing business I was able to observe the negative impact of a newly appointed department head on the shop floor, much as a fly on the wall might. I was inside the organisation but not part of the team or working with them but able to hear and see first-hand what was happening. The new boss, Jane, had a great reputation from the organisations she had worked with previously and was known as a real agent for change. She had been a key member of management teams in organisations that needed restructuring and turning around to survive, and she'd succeeded. The organisation that she had just joined, however, was in a growth phase and required an approach that built on the successes that were already occurring. Jane managed to disenfranchise the supervisors on the shop floor within days of her arrival – quite a feat! Her approach of aggressively analysing processes, and questioning to identify the flaws, didn't acknowledge the great work that was being done to create the current business success. Her turnaround style missed the needs, and she found herself being railed against by her team. Understanding the unique business situation and how that plays to or against your style can be the difference between success and failure.

TIP:

....

Match your style to the situation you're in.

Are you big picture or detailtastic?

For big picture thinkers – Do you find yourself going beyond what is real or concrete and focussing on meaning, associations and relationships?

For detailtastic folks – Do you prefer to take in information using your five senses of sight, sound, feel, smell and taste?

You can't use both methods of perceiving the world at the same time, so you will have developed a preference for using one method over the other.

For each preferred style there will be moments where you are able to do the opposite. So if you are a lover of detail, that doesn't mean you can't see the big picture, and likewise, if you are a big picture person, that doesn't mean you don't get the detail. The real benefit here is to tune in to which is your preference. What comes most naturally to you and which did you have to learn? To have the flexibility to do both is a real skill and being able to adapt ensures greater successes in life. For your choices to be easier and more likely to create success and fulfilment for you, it is important to know what style best suits you and find an environment where it can flourish. For years I worked in the financial field in banking and auditing. As a big picture thinker I managed to learn how to do the detail, and although it was tiring and felt joyless to me I got pretty good at it. Looking back, though, I was not in an environment that encouraged my natural creativity and style. I've only truly flourished since changing profession to one that is less tangible. People and psychology are certainly more ambiguous than accounts. Choosing a profession and how you spend your time by considering how you operate best can be the difference between life feeling easy or hard. Results come faster when you don't have to fight against your natural tendencies. Knowing the things that are most likely to stress you, so that you can create strategies to work around and with them, makes life a whole lot smoother.

If at first glance you would describe yourself as a big picture person, a top liner, for you noticing patterns in things and being able to see the bigger picture comes naturally. So naturally that you may not have even noticed that not everyone does the same thing. Thinking in a metaphorical way or creating ideas and possibilities is simple for you, and being given a blank sheet of paper is the height of excitement. You focus on the end result and create a vision of it in the context of the broadest information available to you. If this rings true for you and you think that this is your style, then you probably also find folks who ask detailed questions quite frustrating. In meetings when questions arise about where the resources are coming from or what the specifics are before you've even got to talking about what is possible, you may find yourself huffing and disengaging.

For top liners, you are most likely to find stress when you:

- Need to focus on past experience (rather than look to the future)

- Have to attend to the details

- Have to do things the 'proven' way

- Are being required to be practical first and foremost

If at first glance you would describe yourself as detailtastic, then being practical, trusting experience and the tangible concrete reality is likely to be your preferred way of approaching things in life. For you the idea of doing something that has no practical purpose feels like an utter waste of time and energy. Why would you spend time theorising and creating concepts if no action were to come of it? Material is most valued when it is sequentially presented and offers the details. You are likely to only want to move into the abstract world of future visions once you have established the current reality. How can you decide where to go if you don't know where you are today? In meetings when people are postulating about the future and 'what if-ing' you may find yourself thinking, "For goodness sake, will you get out of the clouds – let's get real for a moment"!

For detailtastic folks, you are most likely to find stress when you:

- Have to attend to your own or others' insights

- Have to do old things in new ways

- Have to give an overview (without any detail)

- Are looking for the meaning in the facts

- Need to focus on possibilities

- Are faced with too many complexities

Creating a life or choosing roles where you get to do less of the type of activity that your style finds a stressor will reduce your stress. For those inevitable times when you need to apply these approaches, there are two key methods to prepare yourself and avoid the stressor:

1. Surround yourself with people who love the opposite to you (big picture/detail) and are good at it.

2. Practice the methods listed above in times of low risk so you both desensitise yourself to their effects but also build the skills to handle the situation should you need to.

If you find yourself in a role where you are surrounded by many people with the opposite approach to you, here are some tactics you may want to consider employing.

If your preference is for the big picture and your team/work group is detailtastic, consider having a go at the following suggestions:

- Practise offering your information in a step by step, sequential manner (and notice how it is responded to)

- Provide specific examples of vital information so they are based on experience rather than the world of ideas

- Honour your values around experience and tradition

- Read the fine print and make sure to get the facts straight before speaking

If your preference is detailtastic and your team/work group is big picture, consider:

- Getting involved in projects that require some level of future thinking

- Practise brainstorming and ideas-generation (with the rest of the team or friends)

- Choose roles where you get to do less big picture type of activity

- Practise going beyond specifics and begin to create meanings and stories

- Own your strength in the detail and offer your services to the team to be the challenger and pragmatist in meetings

- Prepare yourself for 'roundabout' ambiguous discussions and accept them whilst noticing how useful others find them

- Spend time looking for patterns

By being able to flex your style as well as choosing to be in environments where your natural tendencies are valued, you are setting yourself up to succeed and create the results that you want in life.

STORY

In a corporate employed role before becoming freelance, my CEO, John, was incredibly big picture. He wouldn't listen if you didn't top line your communication in the first sentence, the first 60 seconds! This worked well in many ways in terms of focussing the team's mind and making sure we were succinct, however a lot was lost in the translation. For my first year in the organisation John's style worked well because he had Chris the FD at his side to act as translator. John would speak to the teams, and seemingly, through sheer charisma and his ability to paint a picture with words, he would whip people up into a frenzy. Truly motivated to take action to build the business and take us forward. Then Chris would step in and describe the detail, the operational elements that meant the teams headed out of the room not only fired up but also pointed in the right direction, knowing what the next steps were. Around a year into my tenure with the company Chris left to take on a global role in a large American-owned company based in his home country. We were all sad to see him go and soon realised that his leaving was to have a much greater impact than anyone could have imagined. John continued to be his charismatic big picture self, but the teams were becoming demotivated over time. They no longer had the step-by-step plans, and so the energy that was created had no direction. To know where you are today and where your boss wants you to end up wasn't enough. Frustration grew, and over a very short space of time some of the most talented in the organisation were leaving. It took a change of approach at the top to get us back on track... and John was wise enough to know that he wasn't flexible enough in his style to be able to change fast enough. A new CEO was brought in who, when partnered with the board, had a more balanced approach that offered the teams the direction and operational focus they craved.

The strongest teams have both top liners and detailtastic people in them *and* they value each other's different approaches.

Words are more powerful than the sword

The words you use not only communicate facts but also have an impact on your emotions and your body. Your brain references and connects words to experiences. These experiences come with different levels of tension in the body, different reactions and even different chemicals being released into your body. If you were to take a moment, close your eyes, and imagine that you are taking a bite out of a lemon, the chances are that your mouth will begin to water – totally involuntarily. The way you talk about things either to others or to yourself has an incredible impact on your whole being. Using the power of words to your advantage and recognising the impact they have for you can put you in a really resourceful place – a place where you feel like you have a greater number of choices and the ability to make good ones.

Your language impacts your ability to act

You eavesdrop constantly, maybe not on others but definitely on yourself. What you say to yourself you hear at an unconscious level and it impacts on your levels of motivation, your emotions and your body. What you say can mean the difference between success and failure, no matter what you plan or believe you can do.

Every external event has an internal reaction connected to it. What you experience through your senses is interpreted and processed at a cellular and neurological level. If your skin tells you it's cold, you shiver, if you see something heading towards you at speed, you instinctively get out of the way. It's amazing how quickly the brain processes external stimuli and acts. Your brain filters the information that is coming at it in any given moment and, because of the brain's capacity, sorts to 7 +/- 2 chunks of information. So at best you'll be taking in 9 bits of info and at worst, 5. Of the 2 billion bits of information around you in any given second that's some pretty fast filtering. The bits that get through impact on how you feel and get interpreted by applying language to describe it. This in turn then affects your body. The body-mind connection is literal.

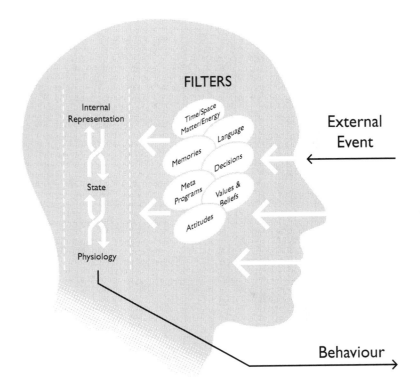

Consider how it might feel to be in a sales team that is told they are at war with the competition. That they must kill the competition at all costs. How would you behave? How much tension would you be holding in your body? Are your shoulders loose as you think about it or tense? Now imagine being in a sales team where your motto and vision is about becoming the world's best – the top of your field – Number 1 in the industry. Notice how different that feels for you. What does that do in terms of your motivation and behaviours? How do you act with the rest of your team? Where do you feel it in your body?

Both these scenarios are ones that I have worked in with sales teams. Both can achieve results. Both also created a different level of internal pressure and stress – the former team had a much higher turnover and sickness levels. They reviewed their goals, and by changing the language from killing the competition to beating them, the culture in the team began to shift. It took some time working with them through observation for the levels of aggression to wane, but together they created a competitive, driven environment that was all about winning, but without the collateral damage associated with the war they had previous felt like they were fighting.

Prefaces and disclaimers

It's likely that you'll have had, or still have, verbal tics that you are completely unaware of. They impact on how you are listened to and how you are perceived. Ever said, "It's just a thought but... " or, "This may be silly but... "? If you find yourself prefacing what you are about to say with this type of statement, you are signalling to your audience (which can be just one person) that what is about to follow isn't worth listening to. You're signalling that you don't believe in what you are about to say so therefore why would anyone else? Single words can have a similar belittling affect. Try these classics on for size – "kind of", "just", "you know". As you hear them, do they add to or diminish the content of what's being said?

STORY

Whilst working as a career coach with Jane, an area manager in a retail bank, we were exploring her personal glass ceiling. Jane was seen as having potential in the bank, she was part of their internal talent programme, and as such had been invested in heavily to keep her and develop her skills. Over the past couple of years Jane had applied for regional level roles in the bank three times and each time she had got to final interview stage but had never been appointed. The feedback she was receiving as to why she didn't get the job was ambiguous and at best pointed towards her gravitas and personal brand. Jane found this highly frustrating as she didn't believe there was anything she could do about it without having to change who she was. As we considered the key stakeholders that had been part of the recruitment decisions, I noticed that Peter had been on the panel each time which got me curious. Jane explained that she had worked for Peter in her last two roles and that he thought highly of her technical skills. As we chatted through how they used to work together a penny dropped, and I began to wonder if the issue at hand was more about perception management than actual reality. Through observation it became clear that language was having a massive impact on how Peter saw Jane in the workplace.

When Jane went to his office she would knock on his open door, wait for him to look up and say, "Come in", and then say something like, "I just need ten minutes, are you free?" Very polite and seemingly harmless in its way. Then I observed those who had recently been promoted where Peter had been involved and they would come to his office, knock, walk in and say something like, "I need ten minutes, you free now or shall I pop back later?" They were respectful of Peter's time and space but more forthright in terms of their request. Jane's polite approach was being interpreted as a weakness. She was being seen as not having the same level of confidence that the others had. It wasn't true, and yet perception is a person's reality, so it was the truth that Peter took into his decision making when deciding who had what it took to operate at a more senior level in the organisation. Having this realization meant that Jane now had a choice to change how she approached Peter on a day-to-day basis. The changes were small but highly significant. Peter's opinion of Jane grew in stature almost overnight. He began bringing her into more strategic level discussions and invited her to play a key role on a global project that the board were about to sponsor. Managing perceptions made a huge difference.

In *Talking from 9 to 5* by Deborah Tannen PhD, her research shows that when it comes to communicating in the workplace, the employees who get heard tend to speak directly, loudly, and at greater length than their co-workers. Being too polite backfires – many people try to avoid seeming presumptuous by prefacing their statements with a disclaimer such as, 'I don't know if this will work', or, 'You've probably already thought of this'. Such disclaimers only cause the rest of the communication to be ignored. For us Brits it's something that we need to be more aware of than most. Our cultural norm is to soften things to a degree that if taken literally doesn't make sense, e.g. "I'm a little bit terrified"! How can you be a little terrified? To be terrified is an extreme state, and if you're not terrified then it's not a little bit of it, instead you are likely to be scared or anxious. Learning to say things as they are without the softeners makes for greater clarity and understanding in our communications.

If you want to change how you or someone in your team are perceived, then simply telling yourself to speak up or telling people in your team to speak up doesn't work in a sustainable way. Some people need time to reflect before speaking and very few people like being told what to do! Companies that want to take advantage of contributions from all employees need to have managers who foster environments that allow for difference. Where are your opportunities to influence this at work? What could you do differently? It could be as simple as letting people know in advance of meeting what's up for discussion.

EXERCISE

....

I say, I say, I say – a linguistic audit

Ask a friend or trusted colleague to listen in when you speak in a different way. Ask them to do a linguistic audit of sorts and to notice any words or phrases that you use in a repetitive way or that have a negative impact on others. Once they give you feedback so you know what they are you can decide whether you want to make a change. Whether you do or don't almost doesn't matter. Now that you know what they are, you will be more conscious of them when you speak and much more likely to notice the impact of them to then make the necessary changes in the moment to be better understood.

....

Once you know something you can't unknow it!

Setting yourself up to succeed

Your brain has a very literal way of interpreting what is being said. It will do what you tell it – exactly what you tell it! For instance, if I say to you "Don't think of a blue tree", what do you think of? Chances are you thought of a blue tree. The reason being that to not think of something you have to know first what it is you are not to think of... so your brain scans your memory files for the thing so that it knows what to avoid. Counter intuitive and yet logical. On a practical level it can be a really useful thing to know about how your brain works. Because instructions are taken so literally, it's important to give instructions that detail what you want and not what you don't want. How often have you said things like, "Don't forget the dry cleaning", or to a child, "Don't drop that," which is often swiftly followed by a crashing sound? It's much more effective to say, "Remember to pick up the dry cleaning," or, "Hold that plate with two hands and be careful". Saying what you want can take practice but it makes a huge difference to what you get in return and it uses less energy.

Remember the last time you heard someone say, "I'll try..." or maybe you've said it recently yourself. When you heard it, how confident were you in that person actually doing what they said they would? It's not the same as if they said, "I'll do it." 'Try' is an interesting use of language to me as it's setting you up to fail. The moment you do the thing you've said you'll try to do you can no longer 'try' so you're not succeeding in achieving the literal goal that you set yourself. I'm suggesting that by saying, "I'll try" you are more likely to fail to succeed. My reasoning here plays to what I've shared earlier about, "Don't think of a blue tree". Your brain is literal by nature. If your brain hears you say "I'll try," then that is the goal... to try! If I say to myself, "I'll try to pick up that jug of water", then the moment I manage to pick it up is the moment I fail because I'm no longer trying – I'm doing. Now with something as simple as picking up a jug of water the chances are your physical abilities will outweigh the linguistic instruction and it'll happen anyway, but with tasks and goals that are more complex or difficult you are giving your brain many opportunities to self-sabotage the task by managing to achieve the goal of continuing to try.

EXERCISE

....

'To Do' list focus

Take a moment and list all the things that you currently have on your 'to do' list that you have framed as "I'll try's". Notice how long they've been there. Ask yourself what would need to happen for you to make this task into an "I will" or an "I must". It may be as simple as changing the language, or it may be that you discover that it's not that important to you so it can come off your to do list... or it may be an area for further exploration as to what's stopping you, at which point I'd advise a conversation with a trusted friend or a coach or taking time out to consider it further.

....

The end …and the beginning

Thank you for taking the time to read this book. It's a real privilege to know that you chose to pick up *Choices* and spend your precious time with it. I hope that you will have taken something new from it, been reminded of some great things you've known already and that you now feel that you have more choices as a result.

Enjoy dipping back into your favourite chapters and exercises whenever the moment feels right. There's an exercise index at the front of the book to help you with that. Know that you now have a resource that you can choose to share, practice from and refer to whenever you need.

So until the next instalment… go and make your life what you want. Bounce back from the inevitable challenges and enjoy the journey.

More Choices

I love to hear inspiring and uplifting stories so do get in touch and share yours. I'm planning to publish *More Choices* later. If you'd like to contribute, then do send them to the address below. I'll make sure, if they are used, that you are credited for your submission.

For information about speaking engagements, workshops, training programmes and coaching, please get in touch. My contact details are below.

Sarah Lane
Coaching Lane Ltd
The Bristol Office
2nd Floor
5 High Street
Westbury-on-Trym
Bristol
BS9 3BY

sarah@coachinglane.com

About the Author

Sarah Lane is an executive and personal career coach, trainer, facilitator, behavioural change specialist and busy mum of a 2 year old. She has spent the last 20 years working in and with people from all walks of life: from chief executives to charity fundraisers, FTSE 100 teams to media creatives. Her love of helping others has always shone through, even in her darker days as an auditor!

Sarah's clients span from local mums looking to balance career and parenthood, to working with organisations including GlaxoSmithKline, MTV, Telefonica O2, The British Red Cross, BMW, Topps Tiles, HSBC and the Fairtrade Foundation.

Sarah brings a pragmatic approach to the psychology of change. She brings a vast and varied business and life experience to her coaching practice. Having qualified and practiced as an auditor, operated in project roles within commercial functions, managed regional sales teams and latterly lead teams in HR and talent management, she connects with her clients from a position of real insight and understanding.

As a coach and trainer, Sarah understands that meaningful change occurs over a period of time. She uses an intuitive sense of what is needed by gathering the facts to be able to hone in on the true heart of issues. Her style works with the knowledge that human beings are multi-faceted by nature, so achieves lasting change with clients by taking a holistic approach and working with the whole person or organisational system.

Originally from Cornwall, Sarah is now proud to also be a Londoner. This is Sarah's debut book, and in true Sarah style she made her choice to write a book, got her head down and completed her first draft in just three months.

7993960R20129

Printed in Great Britain
by Amazon.co.uk, Ltd.,
Marston Gate.